# HOLINESS

# Catholic Spirituality for Adults

General Editor
Michael Leach

Other Books in the Series
*Diversity of Vocations*
*Reconciliation*
*Prayer*

# HOLINESS

⋇

*William J. O'Malley*

Maryknoll, New York 10545

Founded in 1970, Orbis Books endeavors to publish works that enlighten the mind, nourish the spirit, and challenge the conscience. The publishing arm of the Maryknoll Fathers and Brothers, Orbis seeks to explore the global dimensions of the Christian faith and mission, to invite dialogue with diverse cultures and religious traditions, and to serve the cause of reconciliation and peace. The books published reflect the views of their authors and do not represent the official position of the Maryknoll Society. To learn more about Maryknoll and Orbis Books, please visit our website at www.maryknoll.org.

Manufactured in the United States of America.

**Library of Congress Cataloging-in-Publication Data**

O'Malley, William J.
    Holiness / William J. O'Malley.
      p.  cm. – (Catholic spirituality for adults)
    ISBN-13: 978-1-57075-715-0
    1. Spirituality – Catholic Church. 2. Holiness – Catholic Church.  I. Title.
BX2350.65.O43 2008
234'.8 – dc22
                                          2007039765

*For*
*Dr. Charles Rizzo,*
*who brought me back,*
*and for*
*Robert Betterton,*
*who made the trip worth it*

# Contents

# Introduction to
# Catholic Spirituality for Adults

C ATHOLIC SPIRITUALITY FOR ADULTS explores the deepest dimension of spirituality, that place in the soul where faith meets understanding. When we reach that place we begin to see as if for the first time. We are like the blind man in the Gospel who could not believe his eyes: "And now I see!"

Catholicism is about seeing the good of God that is in front of our eyes, within us, and all around us. It is about learning to see Christ Jesus with the eyes of Christ Jesus, the Way, the Truth, and the Life.

Only when we *see* who we are as brothers and sisters of Christ and children of God can we begin to *be* like Jesus and walk in his Way. "As you think in your heart, so you are" (Prov. 23:7).

Catholic Spirituality for Adults is for those of us who want to make real, here and now, the words we once learned in school. It is designed to help us go beyond information to transformation. "When I was a child; I spoke as a child, I understood as a child, I thought as a child; but when I became an adult, I put away childish things" (1 Cor. 13:11).

The contributors to the series are the best Catholic authors writing today. We have asked them to explore the deepest dimension of their own faith and to share with us what they are learning to see. Topics covered range from prayer — "Be still and know that I am God" (Ps. 46:10) — to our purpose in life — coming to know "that God has given us eternal life, and that this life is in his Son" (1 John 5:11) — to simply getting through the day — "Put on compassion, kindness, humility, and love" (Col. 3:12).

Each book in this series reflects Christ's active and loving presence in the world. The authors celebrate our membership in the mystical body of Christ, help us to understand our spiritual unity with the entire family of God, and encourage us to express Christ's mission of love, peace, and reconciliation in our daily lives.

Catholic Spirituality for Adults is the fruit of a publishing partnership between Orbis Books, the publishing arm of the Catholic Foreign Mission Society of America (Maryknoll), and RCL Benziger, a leading provider of religious and family life education for all ages. This series is rooted in vital Catholic traditions and committed to a continuing standard of excellence.

*Michael Leach*
*General Editor*

# Author's Introduction: Accessible Holiness

SENIORS IN HIGH SCHOOL would cringe at being called "holy." The very word secretes poisons like "uninteresting," "sexless," "goody-goody," "unsophisticated." Hardly the path to popularity. Nor does the idea appeal much to older folk. They feel unworthy of a term justified only by a visible halo. Popes can canonize a married couple, but only after thirteen children and late-life vows of celibacy.

Our ideas of holiness are so stringent that even *aspiring* to it seems presumptuous. Jesus faced that. "What's this wisdom that has been given him? Isn't this the carpenter?" (Matt. 13:55). Even slight contact with the un-sacred sullies any suggestion of sanctity. "This man welcomes sinners and eats with them!" (Luke 15:3).

But there is the key: Jesus *loved* imperfect people. On that score all of us qualify!

Therefore, can we consider holiness free of the distancing, antiseptic "requirements" that make the subject — and pursuit of the reality — inaccessible to ordinary folks?

This easing of qualifications seems justified since the scriptures abound with exhortations not just to the few but to the many to strive for holiness. "Be ye holy" (Lev. 20:7; Num.

15:40; 1 Pet. 1:15, 16). "Without holiness no one shall see the Lord" (Heb. 12:14). "This is the will of God, your sanctification" (1 Thess. 4:3). St. Paul's term for *ordinary* believers is *hagioi,* "saints, holy ones." Not just meticulously purified souls but all believers, *made* holy. It is not we who "qualify" as holy, but Christ's generous acceptance of us that negates our unworthiness.

All religious traditions do emphasize the "separateness" of the holy from the everyday. Whatever they call the Ultimate Reality is *totally apart* from anything common, profane, unclean, evil. Jews and Muslims tolerate no pictures of God, lest they devolve into idols. The Reformation ransacked cathedrals and village chapels to purge statues and crucifixes; even the consecrated elements of the Eucharist were desanctified. Eastern faiths go so far as to insist that *no* predicate is worthy of the Deity. Not even "loving" or "intelligent." Indeed, not even "is." Thus, whatever we assert about God is closer to falsehood than truth.

In the Abrahamic tradition, God is utterly *other* than anything created: "I am God and no man, the Holy One in your midst" (Hos. 11:9). Yet God still walked companionably in the Garden with Adam and Eve. There was separateness but also an easygoing connection — until the fateful moment the creatures said, "Who needs you?" And every human since has, in infinitely varied ways, shared that severing arrogance.

Seeking holiness is trying to heal that separation and regain that person-to-Person friendship that makes us holy once again. The very word "religion" *means* "connection."

Most importantly, a constitutive element of Christianity (in contrast to all other faiths) is the *Incarnation*. Uniquely, the Christian God completely enmeshed himself in the material world. "The Word *became* flesh" (John 1:14). Jesus did not feel defiled by what co-religionists judged unclean: neglecting ritual washing or consorting with people considered corruptive: prostitutes, lepers, Samaritans. Moreover, it is also a basic Christian assertion that, except for sin, in Christ God became *fully* human. That means Jesus underwent bodily demands some would consider too degrading for God.

*Can we consider holiness free of the distancing, antiseptic "requirements" that make the subject — and pursuit of the reality — inaccessible to ordinary folks?*

It would also follow that, since of all species *only* humans suffer doubt, the human Jesus had to face the insecurity of commitment to choices without certitude. If not, the temptations in the desert could not have been truly seductive, with no possibility of choosing wrongly. Further, the agony in the garden in which he sweated blood in terror would have been impossible with full access to a divine intelligence that suffers no uncertainty. On the cross when he shouted, "My God, my God, why have you forsaken me?" (Matt. 27:46), he could only have been quoting a psalm, not gripped by genuine temptation to despair. Without experiencing authentic uncertainty,

Jesus simply could not have shared that most difficult burden of being human.

There is at least *one* explanation, though it might not convince all. St. Paul writes that, at the Incarnation, the Son "emptied himself" (Phil. 2:7). He did not stop *being* God, but though he remained fully divine, he surrendered all divine perquisites, like omniscience and omnipotence, *in order* to face life's challenges just like the rest of us.

Jesus' invitation to the Kingdom, a personal relationship with God here and now, was in no way restricted to the special few. In the parable, when the original guests declined, the host ordered: "Go out into the highways and along the hedges, and compel them to come in" (Luke 14:23). It was not restricted to the already righteous: "It is not the healthy who need a physician but those who are sick" (Matt. 9:12). Nor confined to the Chosen People: "Go therefore and make disciples of all the nations" (Matt. 28:19). Nor limited to the ordained Twelve; Jesus "loved" the rich man who "only" lived the commandments but could not leave everything (Mark 10:21). Paul, and finally Peter, flung open the doors indiscriminately: "There is neither Jew nor Greek, neither slave nor free man, neither male nor female; you are all one in Christ Jesus" (Gal. 3:28).

If all that is true, there seems ample justification to examine holiness with less stringent requirements than conventional wisdom might call for. To be judged holy, or at least trying to achieve some semblance of holiness, one need not be flawless, destitute, or virginal. True, to declare publicly someone is a saint, the Church must scrutinize that person's life meticulously. But one need not be a World Series MVP to be judged a legitimate Pop Warner ballplayer.

St. Irenaeus said, "The glory of God is humanity, fully alive." Then it is perhaps permissible to suggest "supernatural" life is not "*supra*-natural," not *beyond* the limits of human nature, but rather humanity itself superbly fulfilled. What separates humans from other animals is the potential to learn and to love. Other animals know facts; a stag pursued by hunters knows that danger is behind him, but as far as we know he doesn't ask *why:* "What did I do to those guys?" We have at least the capacity (if we use it) to understand. Other animals can give their lives for their young. But we can give our lives (often without dying) for people we don't even *like* at the moment. Ask any parent or teacher. Can we entertain the possibility that our God-given purpose is to prepare a fully realized recipient for the gift of holiness? Nor is that role limited to purging defects, as so many were taught, but more importantly it involves amplifying those potentials of knowing and loving. "Let your light shine before men in such a way they may see your good works, and glorify your Father in heaven" (Matt. 5:16).

## Approval

As the book of Job shows clearly, the Architect of the Universe has no need to check his plans with anyone beforehand, not even any official religious body. If God is content that an individual is trying his or her best (for the moment) to fulfill God's hopes in raising humans above animals, that person qualifies as a "saint," even if the Vatican hasn't gotten around to ratifying God's judgment. That person does not even need the external, ritual bestowal of baptism or any other symbolic sign of acceptance (see Simone Weil, Albert Camus, Kurt Vonnegut Jr.). A moment's reflection should make God's unchallengeable assessment obvious, since no intelligent creature would accept a God less kind than oneself.

We all know "unchurched" people who are "the salt of the earth," as Jesus hoped his disciples would be (Matt. 5:13). You can call them when you're stalled on the freeway at 2:00 a.m. They will tell you when you are too pushy or flirtatious or tipsy, and not hesitate because you might stop liking them. Difficult to imagine them excluded from a Kingdom that welcomes the cowardly Simon Peter and the Good Thief.

Nevertheless, it is also clear that it is *easier* for ordinarily self-doubting people if some outside authority validates that inner sense of trying one's best. Baptism and confirmation are incalculably precious assurance of inclusion in a second family that will welcome us back, no matter what. Reconciliation gives a concrete pledge that we can *never* make ourselves so unworthy that we negate what Jesus did for us.

If God so generously offers the merits of Christ to make up for our inadequacies and indiscriminately invites us to holiness, he does not expect anything near undiluted purity of motive or action when he asks us to lead holy lives. This is borne out, page after page in scripture, despite our penchant for sanitizing our saints regardless of what they did.

Abraham, our "father in faith," pandered his wife into another man's harem. Jacob scammed his brother's birthright. Even unassailable Moses stammered for some time trying to weasel out of God's call. David, the model for the Messiah, was a conniving adulterer and murderer. Unthinking piety turns the apostles into bowdlerized saints instead of a passel of Keystone Kops, often bumping into one another in pursuit of personal advancement.

Reflect on down-to-earth holy people you know. Usually not the fastidiously devout, the cautious observers of the tiniest rules, the judgmental. John XXIII, Dag Hammarskjöld, Dorothy Day, Anne Frank. Millions of men and women who refused to surrender their souls in Nazi camps, those who bear with dignity the slow impoverishment of disease, kids crippled in wars they didn't comprehend. The nun who held your forehead when you threw up, the patient teacher who taught you to write, the parents who forgave before we "deserved" it. There is an almost palpable serenity about them. They seem unafraid and open, indiscriminately caring, inwardly coherent and focused. Their holiness is their *wholeness,* their altogether-ness.

The source of that equanimity seems a special relationship with the Ultimate Being and, reciprocally, a freedom from the self-concerned values of "This World." That genuine connection with a transcendent energy source makes them divinely restless, unwilling to ignore or yield to elements of human behavior that conflict with the obvious intentions of a provident God: exploitation, courageous ignorance, neglect of the marginalized, corruption anywhere.

Thus, accepting holiness requires at the very least *conversion* — transformation. Coming to a halt to ask, "Is this the *truth?* Is this where *I want* to go?" Fiercely refusing to be bamboozled any longer by the mesmerizing media that promise instant gratification, then deliver ashes. Rejecting investing your heart and hopes in anything that cannot defy death. Uprooting one's soul, one's *self,* from the trivial and transitory and engrafting it into the eternal.

It is not a static achievement but a continued evolution of soul that, in authentic holiness, becomes contagious. St. Paul suggests ordinary holiness should be easily evident. "The fruit of the Spirit is love, joy, peace, patience, kindness, goodness, faithfulness, gentleness, and self-control" (Gal. 5:22)

If we trim inflated notions of heroic holiness that lead us to negate God's prodigal invitation, we might fulfill the hope that motivated the Incarnation, death, and resurrection of the Son of God: "That you may have life, and have it *more abundantly!*" (John 10:10).

"Be perfect as your heavenly Father is perfect" (Matt. 5:48). Jesus could not have used "perfect" in the sense we ordinarily use it: "flawless, unblemished, absolute." That would have been blasphemous. Only God can be perfect in that restrictive sense. Both Hebrew and Old English meant "perfect" as a sphere, no matter how large or small, is complete.

"Holy" is really a synonym for "successful, fulfilled, well-rounded." Each of those words describes what God intended fully evolved human beings to be. We are the only species which is *in*-complete, whose nature is not an inevitable blueprint but an *invitation.* Every rock, rutabaga, and rabbit fulfills God's intentions without insubordination. They have no choice but to glorify God with an obedience that is, more exactly, helpless conformity. Only we, of all creatures, can choose *not* to live up to the inner programming that invites us by a quantum leap above even the most "intelligent" animals. As far as we know, no shark or tiger is annoyed by qualms of conscience. Animals are incapable of being "wrong."

Those who rise to the challenges of understanding more and loving more at least *seem* more alive, more fulfilled as specifically *human* than those who succumb to the allurements of the Beast in us (pride, covetousness, etc.). Few would argue that Saddam Hussein had a more accurate concept about being human than Sir Thomas More.

Moreover, the requirements embedded in our nature are not immediately operative through inbred instincts. Each of us must *discover* the directions in which we will find fulfillment. This is, or ought to be, the goal of a lifelong education, not merely to make a living but to find out what living is *for.* With that understanding, it becomes more obvious that "holiness" — the full evolution of humanity — is not inaccessible to ordinary people, but it is also not commonplace. It takes a lot of effort.

"Holy" need not be confined to achievement. Just *striving* is enough.

# Chapter One

# The Beyond in Our Midst

*Where shall I go from your Spirit*
*Or where shall I flee from your presence?*
*If I ascend to heaven, you are there!*
*If I make my bed in Sheol, you are there!*
*If I take the wings of the morning*
*and dwell in the uttermost parts of the sea,*
*even there your hand shall lead me,*
*and your right hand shall hold me.*
                                  — Psalm 139:7–10

SINCE THE EARLIEST human days, when our most remote relatives prowled the prairies and forests in search of sustenance, they were apparently aware they were not alone. We know from their burial customs that death held a fearsome sacredness, and they saw death not as an end but a transition to some other unseen dimension of being real, hidden from them here but a reality in which they lived every day. They were, in a real sense, embedded in enchantment. As one Roman poet put it, peering into a darkened grove: "This place is filled with gods!"

Certain places and actions radiated a "specialness" beyond the meaning of the people's humdrum days, and certain occasions — like birth, marriage, and death — held a holy significance. Easy enough to argue that such gullibility arose from primitive lack of sophistication. And yet today even those without religion still find an inner need to express such moments *ritually,* sacramentally, despite their more usual disdain for anything "superstitious." A child's new life, embarking on a precarious future as husband and wife, the emptiness left by a lost parent — such occasions are far too filled with meaning and an elevated sense of importance to be celebrated in some government office or merely with some printed certificate.

Today too even the most urbane of us occasionally are ambushed with our guards down by an onrush of awareness — a sense of being caught up in an occasion "too big to grab hold of": a star-strewn sky, the rhythm of the rain, the harrumph of waves, an infant's fingers, falling in love — and we find ourselves helplessly muttering, "Oh, my God!" Escaping an accident, hearing the "All clear," leaving the hospital where they were sure you would die. Each of those moments has an ecstatic quality wherein we "stand outside" ourselves for a while. We feel, at one and the same time, exhilarated and abased, in reaction to what Rudolf Otto in his masterwork, *The Idea of the Holy,* called "the numinous" — contact with a reality we have not created ourselves, which is actually present to us. Otto names that presence "the *Mysterium Tremendum*": an unknown entity, real and outside the self, which evokes helpless awe in the beholder. It requires an openness to the awesome and by that very fact a wordless admission of inferiority before it.

That awe is not simply an emotion but an intuitional insight into the depth and fullness of our context. Our awareness is not delivered to us through the five practical senses, nor is it the result of logical reasoning. It is more an "intimation," like the sudden flash of certainty one will surely die. We are caught by surprise in such instants because, at least for a brief time, we are "off guard," our regular defenses down. No one can force these intimations to happen; we can only be *open* to them. You are more the victim of this presence than its creator (Carl Jung). Gerald May calls such times of attentive consciousness "unitive experiences"; Heidegger called them *dasein:* really "being there" when you gain authentic elevation as a human being. And unlike momentary highs from LSD or grass, you don't feel let down afterward.

Psychologist William James writes:

> It is as if there were in the human consciousness a sense of a reality, a feeling of objective presence, a perception of what we may call "something there," more deep and more general than any of the special and particular senses.

The poet James Russell Lowell put it more accessibly:

> I remember the night, and almost the very spot on the hilltop, where my soul opened out, as it were, into the Infinite, and there was a rushing together of the two worlds, the inner and the outer. . . . I could not any more have doubted that *He* was there than that I was. Indeed, I felt myself to be, if possible, the less real of the two.

Morton Kelsey sees an affinity between those moments of wonder and the playfulness of children — until formal schooling too often withers their openness and imagination. Indeed, that susceptibility and curiosity accentuate the difference between mere schooling and genuine education, which scoots off in every fascinating direction, like Alice into her wonder-full rabbit hole. It is that quality that enables us to become like children in order to find the Kingdom of God. It is also the quality that raises scientific genius above "mere" technical expertise into the wonderland of scientific discovery: Albert Einstein, Werner Heisenberg, Madame Curie, Carl Jung.

This mystery, which feels more eerie than dangerous, implies three qualities about its numinous, otherworldly cause: first, its elusiveness, that is, its resistance to capture; second, its radiant and humbling purity; and third, its exuberant energy. Those qualities automatically make the beholder feel smaller, inadequate, awed. This is definitely *not* a result of moral guilt for being a sinner, but a "piercing acuteness," Otto writes, "of self-depreciation, a judgment passed, not upon his character . . . but upon his very existence as a *creature.*" It would be at least remotely similar to being invited to play eighteen holes with the winner of the Masters or to dance with the Rockettes. It is almost as if one's own unworthiness would soil the numinous presence.

This indefinable sense of unworthiness *and* connection to the otherworldly is the very essence of religion. Without it, one may claim regularity of religious practice, but the very root of the word, *re-ligare,* means "to bind securely, to connect" with a reality transcending the here-and-now. In a word, to *holiness.* Although painstaking research and reasoning can definitely bring us closer to God, only the subjective experience of person-to-Person encounter will allow God to "prove" himself, just as any other friend does.

> What is contemplative prayer? St. Teresa answers: "Contemplative prayer in my opinion is nothing else than a close sharing between friends; it means taking time frequently to be alone with him who we know loves us."
> (*Catechism of the Catholic Church,* 2709)

The specialness of this union is clearer if you study more frequent events that are only approximations of "the real thing," as in the overpowering experience in a spectacular rock concert or the moment when Rocky Balboa mounts that sweeping stairway of the Philadelphia Museum of Art, and the music surges, and the whole audience wants to cheer! On July Fourth, the Boston Pops playing *The 1812 Overture* with real cannons thundering over the Charles River. It is still difficult not to be caught up in the energy of a vast Nazi Nuremberg rally or the exhilaration at a bullfight, even if you despise what they embody. The whole experience is orchestrated so participants *feel* "outside" the confines of everyday time. One could even include a dazzling performance of the liturgy, surrounded by brilliant stained glass and statuary, swelled with gorgeous chorales — a truly moving experience, but *not* religion without that *connection.*

## God's Grandeur

The world is charged with the grandeur of God.
  It will flame out, like shining from shook foil;
  It gathers to a greatness, like the ooze of oil
Crushed. Why do men then now not reck his rod?
Generations have trod, have trod, have trod;
  And all is seared with trade; bleared, smeared with toil;
  And wears man's smudge and shares man's smell: the soil
Is bare now, nor can foot feel, being shod.

And for all this, nature is never spent;
  There lives the dearest freshness deep down things;
And though the last lights off the black West went
  Oh, morning, at the brown brink eastward, springs —
Because the Holy Ghost over the bent
  World broods with warm breast and with ah! bright wings.

(Gerard Manley Hopkins)

In Alice Walker's *The Color Purple*, Shug Avery, a Depression saloon singer, expresses almost the same insight as Hopkins, a highly educated Jesuit of the staid Victorian era:

I think it pisses God off if you walk by the color purple
in a field somewhere and don't notice it.... People think
pleasing God is all God care about. But any fool living in the world can see it always trying to please us
back.... It always making little surprises and springing
them on us when we least expect.... Everything want
to be loved. Us sing and dance, make faces and give
flower bouquets, trying to be loved. You ever notice

that trees do everything to git attention we do, except walk? . . . Man corrupt everything. He on your box of grits, in your head, and all over the radio. He try to make you think he everywhere. Soon as you think he everywhere, you think he God. But he ain't. Whenever you try to pray, and man plop himself on the other end of it, tell him to git lost. Conjure up flowers, wind, water, a big rock.

*Walking down a corridor at the office or school, pushing through the crowd on a street, we armor ourselves from seeing or hearing — except perhaps the pounding of the iPod.*

Our primitive forebears found the earth more enlivened than we are able to. They had no need for formal study of ecology (*oikos*, our home). They knew instinctively that everything around them was "full of gods," enlivened by a divine spirit: the *Anima Mundi* (Earth Soul). They accepted the truth that we share life with everything on the planet. Native Americans felt that connection profoundly. In 1852, when the U.S. government wrote Chief Seattle offering to buy Indian land, he wrote back:

The earth does not belong to man, man belongs to the earth. All things are connected like the blood that unites us all. Man did not weave the web of life, he is merely a strand in it. Whatever he does to the web, he does to himself.... Your destiny is a mystery to us. What will happen when the buffalo are all slaughtered? The wild horses tamed? What will happen when the secret corners of the forest are heavy with the scent of many people and the view of the ripe hills is blotted by talking wires? ... The end of living and the beginning of survival.

Chief Seattle was a prophet. Now that the wild horses are broken and cellphone towers poke out of every forest, we have become numbed, insulated from our true context. Just so, monkeys raised away from their mothers become sullen and irritable, lost. As early as first grade, school stops being an exploration and becomes the serious business of preparing for college and a high-paying job, which becomes the only operative motive for engaging in the journey of discovery for which God made us. Walking down a corridor at the office or school, pushing through the crowd on a street, we armor ourselves from seeing or hearing — except perhaps the pounding of the iPod. Sometime make up your mind really to *focus* on the faces you walk past day after day and count how many you have never seen before, how much of life you have been missing.

Science says there can be no entity faster than light. And yet science delights in playing, "What If?" What if there *were* an Entity faster than light? It would be moving so unrestrainedly that it would be everywhere at once. Like God. It would be so hyper-energized that it would be at rest. Like God. Some scientists claim that if they finally crack open the tiniest component of matter, what they'll discover is nonextended energy. Like God. $E = mc^2$ means that matter is nothing more than a super-active form of energy!

Couple that with the insight of Exodus (3:14). When Moses asked God his name, he was asking not just for a label but for an explanation of God's role, like the words "baker" or "carpenter." God answered, "I am who am." I am the pool of existence out of whom everything that *is* takes its 'is.' " It begins to appear that science and the Bible are in cahoots! "The world is *charged* with the grandeur of God!"

## The *Shekinah*

*Shekinah* (dwelling, presence) is used in the Targum (Aramaic translation of the Hebrew scriptures) and elsewhere to indicate the presence of God's glory among people. The Hebrew word *shakan* simply means to take up residence for a long period in a neighborhood (Gen. 9:27, Ps. 37:3, Jer. 33:16). It appears as well in the sabbath prayer: "May He who causes His name to dwell [*shochan*] in this House, cause to dwell among you love and brotherliness, peace and friendship." The Talmud asserts that *Shekinah* moves prophets to prophesy and poets to sing psalms. "It" is a wellspring of joy, creativity, and wisdom. The word is a feminine noun and, in the same way that many modern theologians deal with the Holy Spirit, prophets like Isaiah treat the *Shekinah* as a manifestation of the "feminine" in God (Isa. 51:9–10; Wisd. passim). Again, the fruits St. Paul associates with the Holy Spirit are all "feminine," in that Jungian sense of the term: "love, joy, peace, patience, kindness, goodness, faithfulness, gentleness, and self-control" (Gal. 5:22).

God's presence went before the Israelites in their desert wanderings (Exod. 14:20; 40:34–38; Lev. 9:23–24; Num. 14:10; 16:19). When they arrived in Canaan and Solomon finally built his Temple, that presence was so overpowering in the Holy of Holies "that the priests could not stand to minister because of the cloud, for the glory of the Lord filled the house of the Lord" (1 Kings 8:10–13). Matthew's Gospel, written after the destruction of the Temple in 70 C.E., quotes Jesus: "O Jerusalem, Jerusalem, you who kill the prophets, and stone them which are sent to you, how often would I have gathered your children together, even as a hen gathers her chickens under her wings, and you would not! Behold, your house is left to you desolate" (23:37–38). And later, at the instant of Jesus' death, "the veil of the Temple was torn in two from the top to the bottom; and the earth quaked, and the rocks rent" (27:51) as the Presence escaped out into the whole world. Finally, in the book of Revelation: "I did not see a temple in the city, because the Lord God Almighty and the Lamb are its temple. The city does not need the sun or the moon to shine on it, for the glory of God (his *Shekinah*) gives it light, and the Lamb is its lamp" (21:22–23).

Angels too need not to be taken literally when they appear either in the Hebrew or the Christian scriptures. From what we know of the cosmos now, we understand that Gabriel could scarcely use the huge feathery wings he carries in paintings in order to get him from "way out there" beyond the universe, where heaven is, to Nazareth. That is not to deny the existence of angels, only the adequacy of the symbols we use (no matter how ancient and revered) to visualize messages from a God who can communicate faster than light. Nor does questioning the symbols negate the reality, any more than losing an engagement ring means loss of the love it embodies. God can invent anything he chooses, even though we might see no necessity for it, as witness the giraffe, the emu, and the hairy-nosed wombat.

> The existence of the spiritual, non-corporeal beings that Sacred Scripture usually calls "angels" is a truth of faith. The witness of Scripture is as clear as the unanimity of Tradition. . . . St. Augustine says: " 'If you seek the name of their nature, it is 'spirit'; if you seek the name of their office, it is 'angel.' "
>
> (*Catechism of the Catholic Church,* 328–29)

Thus we obviate what become trivial difficulties in scripture like the conflict in the Gospels over the witnesses at Jesus' empty tomb. Matthew has one angel, John has two. Mark has one young man in startling white, Luke has two. Which was it? It hardly matters. A "young man in blazing white" in scripture always meant the same thing: the glorious presence of God. The witnesses were doubled to underline their credibility, as in Hebrew Law.

When the scripture says "an angel of the Lord came," it quite likely meant "when the person encountered the presence of God." In the episode where Moses encounters the burning bush, the book of Exodus clearly identifies the "angel" and God:

There the angel of the Lord appeared to him in flames of fire from within a bush. Moses saw that though the bush was on fire it did not burn up. So Moses thought, "I will go over and see this strange sight why the bush does not burn up." When the Lord saw that he had gone over to look, God called to him from within the bush, "Moses! Moses!" (3:3–4)

Just as it was Yahweh himself who sat with Abraham in the heat of the day, it was he who presented himself to Hagar as she fled the camp (Gen. 16), held back Abraham's dagger over Isaac (Gen. 22), wrestled with Jacob and changed his name to Israel (Gen. 32), and an "angel" is identified with the protective pillars of cloud and fire in the wilderness (Exod. 14:19).

*When the scripture says "an angel of the Lord came," it quite likely meant "when the person encountered the presence of God."*

Consider again the insights of modern science. Neutrinos are singularly elusive elementary particles that have no electrical charge and almost no discernible mass. They arise, allegedly, from atomic decay and travel with such bewildering speed that they can rocket through the whole mass of Earth without being perceptibly slowed. Using the same creative imagination that science uses when playing "What If?" we can ask: What if neutrinos had intelligence and free will? They would have all the properties of angels!

And who is so bold as to say they do *not* have intelligence?

> There are more things in heaven and earth, Horatio,
> Than are dreamt of in your philosophy.   (*Hamlet*)

To become aware of these manifestations of "the Beyond in Our Midst," one has to short-circuit the calculating intelligence that we use to face the problems that devour most of our attention and then reopen the defenseless susceptibility of children within us. As William Blake says in *Auguries of Innocence:*

> To see a world in a grain of sand,
> And a heaven in a wild flower,
> Hold infinity in the palm of your hand,
> And eternity in an hour.

Or as another "innocent" echoed in our own time:

> In the fury of the moment
> I can see the Master's hand
> In every leaf that trembles,
> In every grain of sand.
>                    (Bob Dylan)

Without that freedom to entertain the unlikely, science would be impossible. So too revelation and theology. If we cannot cope with invisible universes-upon-universes within a droplet of ditch water, there is little likelihood we will grapple with the possibility that the Creator of the Universe could shrink himself into an infant in a manger.

Yet when that solely human faculty withers, we are left with the life of Macbeth. Here we stand, hapless, hopeless, hairless apes stranded in a remote corner of a mindless reality

> Tomorrow, and tomorrow, and tomorrow,
> Creeps in this petty pace from day to day,
> To the last syllable of recorded time;
> And all our yesterdays have lighted fools
> The way to dusty death. Out, out, brief candle,
> Life's but a walking shadow, a poor player
> That struts and frets his hour upon the stage,
> And then is heard no more. It is a tale
> Told by an idiot, full of sound and fury
> Signifying nothing.

Or again in the echoes of another modern voice:

> Is that all there is?
> If that's all there is, my friend,
> Then keep on dancing!
> Let's break out the booze and have a ball!
> If that's all
> There is.                              (Peggy Lee)

## A Personal Examen

- Am I really too busy, too scheduled, too concerned with making sure my every minute is occupied with something "worthwhile"? Are there too few times in my week when I pull off to the side of the road and ponder how

I *feel* about my living of my one life? Too few moments of ecstasy — "standing outside" myself, stepping into the eternity I at least claim is the true measure of my meaning?

- Can I recall the last time I felt God ambushing my day? What led me to be caught with my resistance down? If I ever felt sold short because God didn't answer my prayers, did I ever suspect God wanted to be present to me, but he simply couldn't get through my defenses against him?

- The Greek root of both "narcissism" and "narcotics" is the same, *narkoun,* "to benumb." How much of my day is benumbed? The now stale cliché is as true about life as about computers: "Junk in, junk out."

- Make a list of the people in your office, or class, or block, or apartment building. Then ask: How many have I never said hello to? How many can I even put a name to? Which of them consistently looks too preoccupied, or sad, or cheerless, or angry? How would the quality of my living change if I attempted even a surface overture of concern?

- Where are the places where I'm least able to avoid bumping into the presence of God?

- Again and again in the Gospels Jesus went off by himself to pray. What could the Son of God possibly be praying about? Praying for?

# Chapter Two

# Trust

*Then Jesus, crying out with a loud voice, said, "Father, into your hands I commend my spirit!"* —Luke 23:46

THE CLOSEST ANY OF US has ever been, or will be, to paradise on earth is in the womb: warm, fed, floating, secure, "at home," without a care or desire, because we couldn't think. Then, through no fault of our own, we were ejected into cold and noise, then a slap to make us cry—and breathe. And, eventually, think. It was the first in a lifetime of natural crises that summon us to grow more fully human— or not. But the first thing doctors and nurses had to do was clean us up and get us back against the heartbeat that had been our reassurance for the last nine months.

Just so, when a child wakes from a nightmare, alone in the dark, she's completely lost, so she cries out, and almost instantly her mother's there, flicking on the light, hugging her: "It's okay, honey, it's okay." And everything *is* all right again, because out of the darkness has come someone she knows unquestionably can be trusted. She feels at home again, confident again.

When we learned to swim or ride a bike, Dad was there, bigger and stronger than he truly was, assuring, dependable, solid. Only because we were sure the people around us were reliable were we able slowly to develop the *self*-reliance to swim, ride, speak, and move out on our own. All the subsequent natural crises invite us to greater autonomy: playing with kids with different agendas, learning in school the skills to survive, adjusting to a whole new physique and psyche in adolescence. After a while our belief came from within ourselves.

Trust, I suspect, is the *sine qua non* virtue. Without it, slim likelihood we will ever be confident enough to be curious, empathetic, responsible, persevering, because unless we can trust those around us, it's doubtful we will ever truly trust ourselves. Even more problematic that we will rely on a God we can't even see or hear or touch. Without trust (and the ironic union of vulnerability and confidence it can give rise to), no one would ever risk loving.

One need only look at young people (especially young men) who have had no solid figure in childhood against whom to hone their adulthood, like the young man in 1998 who spread HIV virus to dozens of women in southwestern New York State. His grandmother was a crack addict; his mother prostituted herself and her ten-year-old daughter to support her own habit; the boy roamed from one crack house to another with no one to pay him much attention, much less respect. In Freudian terms, he was raw Id, without the slightest taint of a governing Superego. Like fatherless Ishmael, a wandering hunter, set against everyone and everyone against him.

Each of us needs someone we trust to catch us when we fall, but also someone who sees a goodness, a potential, a genuine value in us few others seem aware of. Falling in love is an exhilarating substitute (for a while) when wise parents nudge Hansel and Gretel out of the nest to find their way on their own. At last someone loves me and upholds me when I stumble, cherishing me as uncritically as my parents once did. Romance is an enchanted place to visit, but very few can live there too long. Reality creeps in: Cinderella sometimes has a foul mood; Charming has a tad too much to drink. Even those fortunate enough to discover a spouse who loves them strongly enough to puncture their bluffs often profit greatly from a spiritual director.

*Jesus learned step-by-step, as every human must: how to lace his sandals, how to react to skinned knees, how to defer to clerics, what it meant to be Jesus of Nazareth.*

What a good mentor offers is another ironic coupling: cherishing and challenging, unconditional acceptance joined with a love unafraid to be tough. As a warm-up for depending on God, we have to have parents, or some mentor, who reassures us that everything is all right again, someone who can be trusted unquestionably. Judging from the results, Mary and Joseph provided that for the boy Jesus as he "grew in wisdom, age, and grace" (Luke 2:52).

## Jesus Learning

As we saw in the previous pages, in order to be the model of a Christian's personal evolution, Jesus was *fully* human. St. Paul writes that, at the Incarnation, the Son "emptied himself," freely surrendering the use of divine powers. To adopt a perhaps clumsy metaphor, he became "amnesiac" about who he was so that he could share our confusing human search for a soul and its God-given destination. Jesus learned step-by-step, as every human must: how to lace his sandals, how to react to skinned knees, how to defer to clerics, what it meant to be Jesus of Nazareth.

Jesus obviously was an intelligent boy, as witness his time remaining behind in the Temple with the elders. After that episode, we can only make educated guesses about what kind of upbringing a typical young Jewish boy would have had at that time — weekly religious training, daily lessons in carpentry, but surely none of the specifics.

At his birth, Jesus was truly God, but he no longer knew it. In the same way, each of us is born male or female — objective fact — but it takes us a very long time to grasp even a hazy understanding of what that means. So with Jesus. Just as with each one of us, his lifetime was a series of new insights into who he was.

When Mary taught Jesus how to lace his sandals, she taught him something he genuinely didn't know. When Joseph taught him how to use tools, Jesus was learning something he'd wiped out of his knowledge. When he was lost in the Temple, he certainly showed he was extraordinarily bright. But then at the baptism by John (which immediately precedes the temptations), Jesus had this thunderous realization: "You are the one! The Chosen! You are my Son!" (Matt. 3:17). Who would dare believe that *he* was *the* Messiah? No human being can be prepared for that sort of message. It was . . . impossible.

When you yourself hear the improbable suggestion that you (yes, you!) are energized with divine life, a Peer of the Realm of God, that you must mount the housetops, don't you feel a tad unworthy? Imagine then if you heard what you believed was God himself calling you his Messiah! That's what the Spirit "hurled" Jesus to test in the wilderness, where no divine voices would shield him. And notice the sneering, incredulous tone in each of the temptations: "If you *are* the Son of God, turn these stones into bread!" (Matt. 4:3). Will you get serious? This is a delusion. Take on coercive power! Dazzle them with miracles! You'll have the fools *running* to sign up! Actually fulfill your Father's will! But without the tedious delay. And surely without suffering. Look at all the good you can do! But Jesus refused to do the adequate rather than the best. A hint for all of us who follow him.

For the three years of his public life, then, Jesus went without special help. Remember he always said, "I do nothing on My own initiative, but I speak these things as the Father taught Me" (John 8:28). He had total confidence — faith — in himself, *because* of the Father's confidence in him. Even in the face of demons, Jesus was serene. Faith.

In Luke's Gospel (and only Luke's), at the end of the desert temptations, "When the devil had finished all this tempting, he left him until an opportune time" (*kairos*, Luke 4:13).

Then at the agony in the garden, when he knew his death was a foregone conclusion, he truly panicked. And at the end of his agony, only in Luke, "This is your hour [*kairos*]. This is the power of darkness" (Luke 22:53). From that moment on, all protective force-fields were definitively down. Jesus was out there all alone, without even the felt sense that his Father was with him, with nothing but guts, and *faith*.

On the cross, in torment, he cried out, truly tempted to despair, to doubt that so-certain call at his baptism: "My God, my God, why have you forsaken me?" (Mark 15:34). That's one of the most appealing aspects of Christianity for me: it's the only religion I know whose God was tempted to despair — as I've been tempted to despair. But his final words were: "Father, into your hands I commit my spirit" (Luke 23:46).

What does that say to us? Lots, I think. First of all, like Jesus, we don't comprehend our own greatness, who we really are — sons and daughters of an omnipotent Father. Impossible. Me? I'm nobody. No, you're not. But also we forget, when the sky grows darker and the sea rises higher, that it's perfectly all right to cry out, to bemoan our fate. What's not perfectly all right is to think we *are* out here all alone. It only *feels* that way.

## Discovering What We Have

I am what I am, . . .
And what I am needs no excuses.
I deal my own deck,
sometimes the ace,
sometime the deuces.

It's high time that I
blow my horn and sound my trumpet,
high time, and if
you don't like it, you can lump it.
Life's not worth a damn
'til you can say, "Hey, world!
I am what I *am!*"

(*La Cage aux Folles* *)

Anyone, young or old, who deals with kids, can "tell" which ones are at home inside themselves, who have had a healthy balance of cherishing and challenging. No need to grab attention, prove themselves, seek out caves to hide in; hard-working, at ease. They take their licks with a resigned smile and are above alibis, scapegoating, and requests for extensions. As with the adult Jesus, their parents' wisdom is evident in their personalities.

We can also tell those who have been overly cherished or overly challenged (and in my experience the former outnumber the latter). The unfairly cherished are too often smug, minimalist, indolent; A minds with C averages; their parents fight their battles for them and call them in sick the day of the St. Patrick's Day parade. The unfairly challenged are the nail-biters, the perfectionists, yearning for some (all too momentary) evidence they have value. These are the athletes who come off the losing field punishing themselves for not giving 110 percent (which no one has), the scholar for whom a B+ is an F, as if the Silver Medalist were just Number One among the losers. Such good kids have unconsciously interiorized a conviction that their own parents are unaware they have inflicted on them: If I don't succeed, I won't be loved.

Few of us had two certified saints for parents. No matter what our claims to their sanctity, our mothers and fathers had to have some shortcomings that, for good or ill, affected our unique temperaments, our personalities — what we have to prepare for the gift of holiness.

Without courting blasphemy we can say that the first line of the song from *La Cage aux Folles* could be a translation of the Hebrew *ehyeh asher ehyeh,* the words with which Yahweh answered Moses when Moses asked Yahweh's name, God's function in regard to the People: "I am who I am" (Exod. 3:14). Ancient Hebrew verbs, like *ehyeh,* have no present, past, or future tenses, only a perfective sense (complete, finished) and an imperfective sense (continuing, in process). *Ehyeh* is in the imperfective aspect, and can be construed as God saying he is "in the business of being," that his work is not yet complete, and may never be complete. How do I satisfy Jesus' dictum, "Be perfect, therefore, as your heavenly Father is perfect"? (Matt. 5:48). By *continuing* to *become* more of who I am!

How do I fulfill God's hopes for me? I give glory to God by becoming the best Me I am able to evolve. In the parable of the talents (Matt. 25), the punishment for failing to achieve one's potential, no matter how insignificant compared to those more gifted, is horrific: "And throw that worthless servant outside, into the darkness, where there will be weeping and gnashing of teeth." To claim in trumped-up humility, "Oh, I'm nobody," is cosmically foolhardy!

Who am I, then? And where do I fit into all this? Everybody has a personality; not everybody has character. You can easily see the difference in "He's got a lot of personality" (Robin Williams, David Letterman, Holden Caulfield) and "She's got a lot of character" (Ma Joad, Annie Sullivan, Helen Hayes). Personality is the Me I have to work with, once I come to the age of reason and adult responsibility; character is what I *do* make of that potential. Or not.

*Personality* happens before age three as a series of instinctive responses to influences around us (parents, siblings, playmates, media). A firstborn of nervous parents, for instance, might react to their (indecipherable) anxieties by trying desperately to fulfill their expectations, even before the parents express them: a *defensive* personality. A second child of the same parents could see what a wreck the elder sibling had become and, intuitively, resolve to fight them every step: an *aggressive* personality. Since it occurs without premeditation, long before a child is capable of choice, blame, or merit, personality is no one's "fault" — *except* in what we *do* with that personality once we reach adolescence and afterward. Personality is too often confined to a synonym for "popularity," the external self others react to, whereas the reality is much more a complex of reactive *habits*. *Character* is a series of personally validated and freely chosen *principles*. As such it is definitely premeditated, freely adopted — or not. The morning tabloids and talk shows are unquestionable proof that not everyone develops character. Character is the ethical aspect of one's soul, the true self each of us is when no one is watching: "I wouldn't do that, no matter what they paid me or how badly they threatened me."

The most fundamental difference in personalities is between introvert and extrovert. Extroverts prefer to face challenge in the open, toe-to-toe; introverts are more comfortable withdrawing to a quiet place and pondering. The first question is, most basically, am I a battler or a brooder? Or an interesting mix of both? Like being left- or right-handed, neither is "better." Each has clear assets and liabilities. The important thing is to use the personality's resources well and control its vulnerabilities. Even more important is to realize, and accept, that a personality type is not an inherited, incurable disease. Too many offer limp alibis for their unhealthy habits: "Oh, I guess I'm just a procrastinator. . . . I've always been shy (or pushy). . . . I've never been able to take responsibility for my stupid actions. But I blame my parents for that." They blame their faults on their personalities instead of blaming their personalities on their faults. We are not prisoners of habits we formed unconsciously as children, any more than an alcoholic is a helpless "victim" of his addiction. The crucial point is that a timid person can become confident and outgoing; an aggressive person can become thoughtful and considerate — without abandoning the advantages of their former habits. But it takes effort!*

---

*For a very sketchy understanding of at least nine personality types, possibly the most thorough and most accessible study is Don Richard Riso, *Personality Types* (Boston: Houghton Mifflin, 1987). For a free, automatically interpreted test, log on to *www.9types.com/rheti/homepage.actual.html*. For a good, relatively compact introduction, see *www.enneagraminstitute.com*.

The crucial life-task of adolescence (which far too many miss on the way through, in the welter of fashion magazines, competition, and popularity ploys) is to discover and accept a unique identity, a *self*. That process of emerging as an adult in adolescence is, by nature, requisite preparation for offering that appropriated self to another in the intimacy and partnership of marriage. Then in the natural order of things, the couple begins to have children, whose very spirits depend on the character of the parents and on the solidity of their union. All of which is strong evidence that the primary task of schools and parents is not to ace the SATs and get these children into good colleges, not to prepare attractive job candidates or even good citizens, but to cultivate good spouses and parents. If those who empower the young succeed in that, all those other goals will take care of themselves.

*Character is the ethical aspect of one's soul, the true self each of us is when no one is watching.*

What do you find when you look within? A neglected pawn shop of feelings, notions, fears, convictions? A snarl of synapses and reflexes? A vipers' tangle of resentments, wounds, unfocused anxieties? The *essential* first step is to clear out the useless junk: the "if only's," because whatever follows those two words is one of "the things that *can't* be changed." Just like cleaning out a long-ignored attic, pausing to ponder all those contrary-to-fact yearnings is so hypnotic that all the clean-up time is lost: "If only I had a different set of parents.... If only I had a different skin color.... If only I'd been born rich (beautiful/athletic/smart — fill in any value huckstered by commercials).... If only I hadn't *done* that!" Unless you begin at the rock-solid, painful *truth,* you're pumping your legs like Elmer Fudd long beyond the cliff's edge. There's only two directions you can go: straight down to a smash-up or back to the drawing board. "I am what I am, And what I am needs no excuses."

No matter how unfairly Fate has treated me, the only sane posture is: "Okay, 'they' have blasted my psyche to bits. Now what can I build from this rubble?" We must resolve to get out of God's way in his desire to make us holy.

Besides "if only's," there are a legion of ways to avoid building character. Defensively, there is scapegoating, laying the blame on the economy, siblings, "Society." The only honest counter-ploy is: "Okay, how do I circumvent that?" Another is minimalism, getting by with the least effort, just mop where the boss can see, filling space with words. Does that kind of evasion make you *happy?* Kahlil Gibran wrote: "Work is love made visible. And if you cannot work with love but only with distaste, it is better that you should leave your work and sit at the gate of the temple and take alms of those who work with joy." Withdrawal is equally self-destructive, credit cards won't come due for a while, I've got enough friends, I'll wait till... when?

Avoidance of one's true self can also be offensive (in both senses). Masks that try to disguise the absence of a self inside: "expressing myself" by imitating someone else, resorting to plastic surgery — or at least every panacea on TV, paying extra to become a walking billboard for Nike or Nautica. "I am what I am. What you see is what you get." Competition can also block us from our true selves: "Look at those pecs, *huh?*... What do you think he's worth?... No raise. Do they want me to quit?" Against these one can only stand firm: "I gave them my best." And one of the worst faults of genuinely good people is perfectionism: "If only I'd given 110 percent.... It seems so easy for everybody else.... I'll never get it, so why try." If you really want to be humble, ask for help. Till then, "My best is all I have and, for now, it has to be good enough!"

*"Okay, 'they' have blasted my psyche to bits. Now what can I build from this rubble?" We must resolve to get out of God's way in his desire to make us holy.*

In *The Screwtape Letters* by C. S. Lewis, an arch-devil named Screwtape sends dispatches to his nephew, Wormwood, who is on his first recruiting mission. They are filled with satanically shrewd advice. You don't have to turn them into potentates of porn or serial killers, Screwtape advises. All you need to do is give them a *mirror!* Whether they're mesmerized by their own beauty or ugliness doesn't matter. As long as they're focused on themselves, they're paralyzed, of no use to The Enemy. On the other hand, an equally wise truth was etched in gold on the lintel of the Oracle at Delphi: "*Gnothi Seauton* — Know Thyself." Without false humility, without false *anything,* we have to scrutinize ourselves, maximize all our assets and minimize our liabilities so that we can personally *own* that self. Then, confident in that self's radical worth, we have to get on with the business of living.

> God grant me the serenity to accept the things that can't be changed, the courage to change the things that can be changed, and the wisdom to know the difference.
>                                          (Reinhold Niebuhr)

The only antidote to the narcissism (self-absorption) and inertia (unwillingness to change) that we inherited from our simian forebears is simply *honesty.* Narcissists tell themselves lies, about themselves, and, tragically, believe them. "I'm an honest man. I cheat only when I have need and opportunity."

No one said the truth would make you giggle. Just set you free.

## A Personal Examen

- Do I really give the Wolf within me his or her due? In the interests of decorum and others' expectations have I in a true sense kept a significant aspect of my total self stillborn? Any virtue, without the corrective of its opposite, can slip unnoticed into a vice. Is that true of caution and spontaneity in me?

- List the people — from life or from history or from fiction — who you personally believe qualify for The Best of Our Species. Jesus is a good start, but there are surely many, many more.

- Make an X where you think you are now.

Introvert ←——————————→ *Extrovert*

Anti-intellectual ←——————————→ *Intellectual*

Indifferent ←——————————→ *Inquisitive*

Wary ←——————————→ *Trusting*

Fluctuating ←——————————→ *Decisive*

Self-protective ←——————————→ *Self-giving*

Discouraged ←——————————→ *Cheerful*

Resentful ←——————————→ *Forgiving*

Worldly ←——————————→ *Spiritual*

Where do you think you need to move some of those X's to the right or left? How?

- The agony in the garden and Jesus' cries from the cross manifest a truly human, evident confusion, yearning to be consoled. If I take my confusions to him as if I were with him in one of those places, he most likely will offer no "answer." But does the simple sharing with a Fellow Sufferer ease the aloneness?

# Chapter Three

# Honesty

*Simply let your "Yes" be "Yes," and your "No," "No."*
— Matthew 5:37

THE GLUE THAT holds together our web of moral relationships (society) is trust. I need at least some vague conviction *most* people on the bus with me are not packing guns, or at least won't use them. A quarterback has to trust that his linemen aren't going to flop down and let the opposition mangle him. When an actress finishes her solo, she has to believe the people who are supposed to come on stage and continue the show will not leave her out there swinging slowly, slowly in the wind. Without trust, we become a nation of justifiable paranoids.

But trust dovetails right into honesty. "Whoever can be trusted with very little can also be trusted with much, and whoever is dishonest with very little will also be dishonest with much" (Luke 16:10). If I know from experience someone will lie when the cost of honesty is relatively trivial (a scowl from some authority), I have at least to suspect that, if the cost of honesty were extreme (losing your driver's license for a year), that person is "a hostile witness." Conversely, if

they habitually come right out and admit they've screwed up
when they have, I'll tend to believe them when they say they're
innocent but the evidence seems to suggest they're not. Even
with no relation to religion, a habit of honesty is in anyone's
own self-interest. Nobody's ever going to "catch you out" if
you always tell the truth. And it's easier to remember!

As trust dovetails into honesty, honesty grafts itself into
the truth. The truth is "out there" before it's in my head or
in my words. What I say is legitimate and reliable only if objective evidence backs it up. Therefore, if the fabric of society
depends on trust, and trust depends on honesty, and honesty
demands the truth, one might say without exaggeration the
whole purpose of education (vs. schooling) is to enable people
to learn how to *see and speak and do the truth*.

Moreover, the objective evidence, things as they truly are,
*manifests* the will of God, etched right into the way every
single thing is made. They tell me what they are and how
God intends me to use them legitimately. A rock and a potato
may look exactly alike, but the potato tells *me* I can bite it,
and the rock tells me I can't. Therefore, there's something objectively wrong, defiant of God's will, in lobbing food around
in a food fight as if it had no more internal value than a
snowball. A puppy tells me, by the way it reacts, that it has
feelings, unlike any cabbage, and therefore there is something
objectively wrong in setting a dog on fire as I could reasonably do with a Christmas pudding. Something within human
beings, their power to understand and love, makes it undeni-
ably wrong to raise human babies to eat, as we can licitly do
with calves. That evident difference makes it clearly wrong

to use another human being as a casual release for my sexual tensions, as other animals may. As far as we know, no orangutan kills herself because her mate consorts with other females. Humans do; we set justifiable expectations of others that no other animals can. Any honest person needs no written laws from Church or State to know that. Laws are written for people too dumb or too self-blinded or too egoistic to figure that out for themselves!

> It's who you are and the way you live that count before God. Your worship must engage your spirit in the pursuit of truth. That's the kind of people the Father is out looking for: those who are simply and honestly *themselves* before him in their worship. (John 4:23)

The will of God calls me not merely to see the truth but to *yield* to it, even when the Beast still within me wants to blot out the truth, deny the truth, change the truth into something false but more palatable. Truth is the only antidote to narcissism, to animal self-absorption. The psychiatrist Carl Jung made clear that all neuroses — anxiety, obsessional thoughts, compulsive acts — are rooted in an inability or refusal to yield to objective truth. No need for hell to punish those who refuse to accept the facts; misery is built right into that refusal.

Yes, my husband left and *won't* come back; yes, I *did* lose my leg; yes, I *was* mean to my friend; no, I *can't* make him love me as much as I love him; no, I *can't* treat gin like ginger ale for very long without suffering. Facing the truth, flat on, is often very painful, yet the neurotic games we fabricate to avoid the unchangeable truth are always more bitter, more confusing, and more self-destructive than yielding to the truth would have been.

*Even with no relation to religion, a habit of honesty is in anyone's own self-interest. Nobody's ever going to "catch you out" if you always tell the truth. And it's easier to remember!*

The first step toward wisdom, and true freedom, is to call a thing by its right name, to be honest with *yourself.* If this sexual action is (judged at the most honest depth of yourself) not in the same class as a mother's self-forgetful love for her baby, but just a self-indulgence, don't call it "making love." Call it by the other word. It may be uncomfortable, but it will be the honest truth. My daughter is not "just high-spirited and popular"; she's well on her way to becoming an alcoholic. If I don't stop being so inflexible, my own children are going to have good reason to hate me. Kid everybody else, but surely don't kid yourself, about yourself. If you refuse, the retribution is inevitable.

Aristotle said we learn virtues by doing them; he could have said the same about vices. The first little lie is uncomfortable; the next one is easier; finally, it's hard even to be aware that we are, in fact, lying. We have a nearly infinite capacity to kid ourselves, to assure ourselves we're honest when we routinely cheat when honesty is bothersome, to tell ourselves we are loving when we destroy other people's reputations without a thought, to pride ourselves with being loyal when we don't give an honest day's work for an honest day's pay. They tell a story (too good to be true) about George Bernard Shaw sitting next to a voluptuous blonde at a dinner. He twitches his mustache and asks, "I say, would you sleep with me for 100,000 pounds?" She blushes demurely and responds, "Well, I rather think I would." He snickers, "Would you sleep with me for five pounds?" She pulls herself up and snaps, "*What* do you think I *am?*" He snickers again and says, "We've settled what you *are*. Now we're just haggling over prices."

People often object that telling the truth, being honest, is sometimes too hurtful, not just to the speaker but to the one spoken to. That is a just objection. When a friend asks how you like her dress, and you think it's dreadful, the only kind reply is something playful like "You make anything look great." If she pushes further, answer: "If you like it, that's all that counts, right?" If she starts getting hotter, then she deserves the truth. She asked for it. The *Catechism* says:

> Charity and respect for the truth should dictate the response to every *request for information or communication*. The good and safety of others, respect for privacy, and the common good are sufficient reasons for being silent about what ought not be known or for making use of a discreet language. The duty to avoid scandal often commands strict discretion. No one is bound to reveal the truth to someone who does not have the right to know it. (2489)

There is also an old moral chestnut that says, *non expressio falsi, sed suppressio veri,* not expression of a falsehood but withholding the truth. It's the basis of the Fifth Amendment: "I refuse to answer on the grounds it might incriminate me." Prosecutors have to prove your guilt by other means; by law they can't expect you to convict yourself when they're unable to. In the ludicrously tragic McCarthy hearings, witnesses were asked if they were now or ever had been communists. Many "took the Fifth" simply because they believed the bases for the question were not only irrelevant to their loyalty as American citizens but an abuse of their inalienable human rights. If a stranger asks you how much money you're carrying, it's none of his business.

*Facing the truth, flat on, is often very painful, yet the neurotic games we fabricate to avoid the unchangeable truth are always more bitter, more confusing, and more self-destructive than yielding to the truth would have been.*

In Elizabethan England, when harboring a Catholic priest was legally treason, those guilty of doing so simply answered no when asked if they were hiding a priest, since they believed in their deepest conscience the law was immoral and therefore the questioner had no moral right to a true answer. They defended themselves in court with a hypothetical case: "Suppose

I were hiding the Queen from assassins. Would the court force me to tell the inquirers that I was not?" The same argument would defend those who hid runaway slaves in the antebellum South and Jews in Nazi Germany. No matter what a country's laws, it is also immoral to threaten a lawyer, psychiatrist, or minister of religion if they refuse to breach confidence.

## The Way

> I am the way and the truth and the life. No one comes to the Father except through me. (John 14:6)

At his temptations, Jesus rejected all subterfuge, all weaseling with words. Where the negative commandments of the Old Law left plenty of room for loopholes, his New Law sealed off all avenues that justify self-deception. A man once told me it was okay for him to visit prostitutes because the commandment says, "Thou shalt not commit adultery," and he wasn't married. He might also have said he was permitted because he wasn't an adult! "Love your neighbor as you love yourself" has no such soft spots.

When a lawyer tried to test Jesus on the meaning of "eternal life" (human purpose), and Jesus answered that it meant loving God by loving one's neighbor, the lawyer "wanted to justify himself, so he asked Jesus, 'And who is my neighbor?' " (Luke 10:29). Jesus saw through his ploy: The man was asking, "Whom can I *exclude?* Surely you don't mean the corrupting outcasts the Mosaic Law allows us, in fact *orders* us, to shun?" Jesus was above trickery, but he was no one's fool. "Be shrewd

as serpents but gentle as doves." He knew intuitively that had
he spoken the truth flat out (that God wants *no one* excluded),
the lawyer would have snorted and gone on his way.

So he answered the question with a story about a man trav-
eling to Jericho who was set upon by thieves and left to die in
a ditch. Deftly, Jesus tells the story from the Jewish *victim's*
point of view and expectations: the holy priest, the layman
in Temple service, and then of course (since such stories
always have three characters) the audience expected an ordinary good lay person like themselves. But no! A Samaritan!
The victim wouldn't even *want* such a renegade's help. Like
Al Sharpton looking up into the face of the Grand Dragon of
the Ku Klux Klan. But in the circumstances....

St. Thomas More used the same cleverness — up to a point.
In *A Man for All Seasons,* he says:

> God made the angels to show Him splendor, as He made
> animals for innocence and plants for their simplicity.
> But Man He made to serve Him wittily, in the tangle of
> his mind. If He suffers us to come to such a case that
> there is no escaping, then we may stand to our tackle
> as best we can, and, yes, Meg, then we can clamor like
> champions, if we have the spittle for it. But it's God's
> part, not our own, to bring ourselves to such a pass. Our
> natural business lies in escaping.

Nonetheless, there are times, as More and Jesus himself
finally found, when we can no longer finesse. Let no one find
refuge in mealy-mouthed assertions about Jesus, like "he was
one of the finest moral teachers who ever lived." Jesus didn't

leave us that option. At his trial before the Jewish elders, the high priest asked him, forthrightly and with no room to maneuver, "*Are* you the Christ, the Son of the Blessed?" *Are* you the Messiah, on a level with the Divine Lord?" And Jesus answered with equal forthrightness, "I AM!" (Mark 14:61–62). He had taken to himself the unpronounceable name of Yahweh. In John's Gospel, he says the same, "I tell you the truth," Jesus answered, "before Abraham was born, I am!" (John 8:58). And "The father is in me, and I am in the Father" (John 10:38). At that, the high priest tore his garments in fury. "We have no more need of witnesses! You've heard his blasphemy" (Mark 14:63–64)! He's condemned himself out of his own mouth. To give credit to those who executed Jesus, they weren't fools enough to put to death an irrelevance who wanted only that we be kind to one another.

"What is truth?" Pilate asked (John 18:38). Then he sent it to be crucified. Not for the first or last time.

## A Personal Examen

- What are the concrete predicates I add to phrases like "I want to...," "I'd like to...," "I wish..."? Do I really want those things? Or are they just wishful thinking? Merely frustrating "if only's"? Am I deceiving, and therefore bedeviling, the one person in the world I dare not mislead?

- Have I ever been in an argument, when suddenly a light popped on in my head, and I said, "Rats! They're right!" — but I kept on arguing? Why? It certainly wasn't that I really wanted to find the truth, right? What kept me going? Probably the fact that "winning" was more important, or at least not having the appearance of losing. I don't want to look stupid. And yet the longer I argue when even *I* know I'm wrong, the stupider I look!

- In the middle of President Clinton's second term, the nation was smothered with a nit-picking investigation of his alleged sexual misconduct that seemed to go on forever. The special prosecutor was as relentless as Javert in *Les Misérables*. When the evidence finally became inescapable, the president of the United States defended his weaseling his way past a grand jury by saying, "It depends on how you define 'having sex.' " What would have happened — to his own reputation, to the office of the presidency, to the confidence of the nation, and to the moral state of society — if, as soon as the accusation had been made public, he had gotten on national television and made the same apologetic and remorseful speech he finally was forced to make (even after his first nationally aired, half-hearted admission)? What does that say to me?

- When I approach the Sacrament of Reconciliation, do I still spend too much time before approaching a confessor, trying to find the most "neutral-sounding" words, hedging, leaving the priest to figure out what "I did bad things" actually means? Whom do I deceive? The priest? God? Myself? How different would I feel emerging from the sacrament just as from the final defenseless struggle with the dentist?

# Chapter Four

# Impartiality

*He causes his sun to rise on the evil and the good, and sends rain on the righteous and the unrighteous.*

— Matthew 5:45

ONE WINTER when I was teaching in upstate New York, we had eight consecutive snow days in early January. No one could get out of the house, even to the store. It got pretty claustrophobic; family members were close to matricide, patricide, fratricide, sororicide, and suicide. Among other diversions. Because we had lost so many school days, the administration decided to cancel the Presidents' Week vacation. Bad move. The tensions built back up again, this time in the school. Pranks escalated to the point of serious harm. So at a teachers' meeting, a couple of us suggested we cancel the three days before the Easter break and have a full two weeks to let all the strain ease off. But the physics teacher was adamant. "If I lose those three days," he said (pretty intensely), "I won't be able to get to *magnetism* at the end of the year!" I said I supposed somebody taught me magnetism in my senior year, but I couldn't remember a single thing about it, and therefore no one would be *that* impoverished to miss it. We argued on and on, but eventually his opinion prevailed. (And the following year he became principal.)

At the root of all that's wrong with the school system is simply that: missing the forest for the trees. It becomes imperative that we "cover" magnetism. Doesn't matter if anybody finds it useful, important, or worth remembering. It's "on the syllabus" and therefore as unchallengeable as death. Some graduate from high school without having read *Hamlet* or *Lord of the Flies*. They've missed some interesting stuff, but as long as they've learned how to enjoy increasingly more challenging material and understand it, they've done just fine. Some graduate without calculus, but they don't need calculus to create a budget or balance a checkbook. As long as they can cope reasonably with complicated numbers, they've done just fine. But those fundamental skills are only the most basic *tools,* like learning to hammer a nail or fit pipe — essential as a start, but hardly enough to build a house. Once you've mastered the basic skills, you're ready to *begin.* The true task of education, no matter what the forgettable specifics like magnetism and *Hamlet,* is learning how to *reason to honest decisions.*

The same, more's the pity, holds true for religious education. Encyclopedic coverage of every doctrine seems to be critical, and as early as possible before kids escape it, even though it in no way impinges on the felt needs of those taught and therefore is even less memorable than trigonometry. Why little kids need to hear of the Virgin Birth years before they're aware of what sex means begs justification. Knowing *about* the God questions becomes more needful than knowing *God*. Another result is that all doctrines seem to carry the same weight, rather than being a spectrum of tenets ranging from the essential (like the Incarnation and abortion) through the important (like worship and grateful service), to the trivial (like maniples, St. Christopher, and communion by intinction).

All this may seem considerably distant from the pursuit of holiness. But until one can think honestly and critically, one is a helpless prisoner of the last, loudest voice, the most persuasive huckster, the one who tried to misdirect Jesus at the very outset of *his* mission. Clear thinking is definitely an essential to beginning theology, which is not for children. And although theology is not a requirement to holiness, it can surely be an obstacle to it.

Reasoning to impartial decisions means forming one's own personally validated opinions rather than going with "Everybody says...," or "Society tells us we have to...," or even "the Church says I must...." It definitely does not mean denying what authorities prescribe but rather asking why they believe such-and-such is true before I accept it as true. God gifted us with minds which he gave to no other animals *before* he gave us authorities, and we can conclude he intended us to use them to fulfill our human purpose. Arriving at personal convictions requires that we (1) gather all the pertinent evidence (without ignoring unpleasant applicable evidence), (2) sift out the most important (most of your research you'll never use), (3) put the best evidence into a logical sequence (if you don't know how to outline, you don't know how to think), (4) draw a conclusion (the report, the essay, the editorial, the recommendation), and (5) submit it for a critique to someone more experienced (the teacher, the boss, the IRS, the judge).

There is the reason for education: (1) gather, (2) sift, (3) outline, (4) conclude, (5) critique. If you got away with a slip-shod job at that first time through, it's never too late.

Every time we arrive at a decision, each of us acts as a judge, whether the matter for decision is trivial (a movie or bowling, balanced diet vs. junk food), or whether the matter is very important (commitment to this spouse, deciding if a particular relationship really legitimates genital expression). In cases all along that spectrum, and with increasing importance as the questions become more consequential, we have to ask ourselves to be, like any judge, impartial.

Ah! There's the rub. An honest, impartial judgment has to be free of bias, which can come about in any number of often undetected ways — even under the guise of obedience, loyalty, or love. Think of Tevye in *Fiddler on the Roof,* treating the daughter he loved fiercely as if she were dead because she broke the Law in marrying a Christian. Consider guards in extermination camps who did the unspeakable because they were "only following orders." Ponder the sister who lies to protect the dope-dealing brother she loves rather than defending his victims. However costly their convictions, their complete loss of perspective made them feel righteous.

We will consider only four basic obstacles to impartiality, plus their indispensable servant: reductionism. The most obvious hindrances are (1) ingrained prejudice, (2) inadequate study of the alternatives, (3) vested interests, and (4) uncritical acceptance of false propaganda.

## 1. Prejudice

Bigots — of whatever race, creed, social class, ethnic origin — have rock-hard opinions based on no evidence but hearsay, crowd-think, or unexamined "traditions." What's worse, they *act* on their ill-founded beliefs: lynch mobs, terrorists, street gangs, SS troopers. Racial and ethnic groups detest one another because "they" are taking "our" jobs. For four hundred years the Northern Irish have been killing one another over a religion neither side seems eager to practice. Many of the wealthy scorn those on welfare, and many of those on welfare despise the wealthy because they're the reason for welfare. What all these closed-minded folk deny is that, beneath our differences, each one of us is equally *human,* with exactly the same hopes and rights, which our humanity (not the Declaration of Independence) confers on each of us: life, liberty, and the chance to pursue happiness. And if every human has a right to life, he or she also has a right to those goods without which life is impossible: food, clothing, and shelter. Objective facts. Unlike bigots, most of us console ourselves with the belief we are open-minded, generally without serious prejudice. But check that belief with complete honesty and impartiality. Are there not a few "types" for whom we haven't the slightest fellow-feeling, who in fact make us cringe? What about grossly overweight people? Loud-mouthed, know-it-all jocks? Painfully shy people? What about homosexuals?

I find very little trouble opening my heart and hands to the destitute of body and soul, the leprous, the prostitutes, the Samaritans. The gifts I've been given were so undeserved, empathy with the less fortunate is axiomatic. What man with any decency could withhold it?

Ah, but there still remain those to whom my soul seems resolutely locked. I find it nearly intolerable to open my heart to any kind of humorless puritan or literalist. I have no forbearance for hyper-Catholic types who belabor the bishop with my every slightest departure from the Roman Ritual. I find no forgiveness for well-fed colonels and managers and supervisors who fire off unquestionable orders to the front when they haven't faced live ammunition themselves in twenty years. I still have a great deal of work before I'm ready for the unresentful joys of heaven.

And of course all those nit-picking demons I welcomed obediently in my childhood and nurtured for years came swarming home after the psychic housecleaning. I'm shamed that I'm still irritated way out of proportion by my fellow pilgrims' trivial eccentricities. I must learn to smile when someone asks me how I'm doing at seven in the morning. I have to remember that adolescence *is* curable when I find gum in a drinking fountain or a kid continues to argue long after even he knows he's wrong. And I must learn to forgive that worst of all petty narcissisms: leaving the toilet roll empty.

Are they all persons, just as — and just as much as — we are? Do we sense their need for attention, respect, even understanding? Even if we did sense some kind of fellow-feeling for those "unacceptables," would our need for our friends' approval keep us from striking up a friendship (or just a conversation) with one of them? If not, there's little room for the wide-open vulnerability of "Love your neighbor as you love yourself."

---

*I find it nearly intolerable to open my heart to any kind of humorless puritan or literalist. I have no forbearance for hyper-Catholic types who belabor the bishop with my every slightest departure from the Roman Ritual.*

---

There's no assignment of guilt here, just an honest assessment of one's own impartiality of judgment. Once someone accepts that, he or she can start to rectify it. That's what learning is for: to prepare for making honest, impartial decisions — especially about people.

## 2. Inadequate Study

A severely limited point of view (or perhaps more forthrightly, "courageous ignorance") is poor basis for impartial judgment. Any inquiring-reporter column proves beyond question that everybody in the country has an opinion on any question under the sun: the coach of the Knicks, the effects of secondary smoke, the morality of abortion, welfare, extramarital sex. But precious few have actually reasoned their answers out for themselves (gather, sift, outline, conclude, critique). Or read a book on the topic. Even one book is hardly enough for any complex question, since books themselves are often biased. But one book is far better than no serious consideration at all, and surely better than "I know this guy . . . " or "I saw a TV show once . . . " or "Everybody knows. . . . "

Chesterton wrote that the Church is not like a sleek pillar but like a huge, ungainly, knobby rock whose bizarre outcroppings balance one another over the years.

> The instinct of the Pagan empire would have said, "You shall all be Roman citizens, and grow alike; let the German grow less slow and reverent; the Frenchmen less experimental and swift." But the instinct of Christian Europe says, "Let the German remain slow and reverent, that the Frenchman may the more safely be swift and experimental. We will make an equipoise out of these excesses. The absurdity called Germany shall correct the insanity called France."

Any virtue, unbalanced by its opposite, runs amok into a vice. Innovation without caution becomes chaos; caution without innovation becomes sterility. Justice without mercy devolves into vengeance; mercy without justice results in spinelessness. Conservatives and liberals *need* the balance afforded by the other.

### 3. Vested Interests

When a conflict arises over any issue, trivial or grave, legal or moral, you're not going to get a fair trial when the judge has something to lose by being impartial. Discuss the effects of smoking with the CEO of a tobacco company, or welfare with someone who pays heavy taxes, or what legitimizes sexual activity to an already sexually active teenager, you can be sure the other side is going to maximize the evidence that supports them and minimize (or outright ignore) any that threatens them. We would prefer to see ourselves as virtuously impartial, free of bigotry, tolerant of "differences." But in our objective moments we must admit we are tempted to be quite partial in judgment of our own motives.

One needn't be a professional historian or theologian to see that what have been casually designated "religious wars" (an oxymoron if there ever was one!) were motivated far more by economic factors, stubborn arrogance, and bruised feelings than by sincere theological beliefs.

### 4. Uncritical Acceptance of False Propaganda

No Inquisitor, no cult master, no Gulag brainwasher could hope for the sponge-audiences now presumed by the media: TV, rock lyrics, the glossy mags. Probably most people are no longer genuinely free after dinner to play Monopoly, sew, do carpentry, go for a walk, read a book. Like automatons, we head for the couch and the remote: "I hear and obey!" The TV programs and commercials "tell" us, without a direct word being said, that "the more things you have, the happier you'll be." (The best brainwashing is the brainwashing you'd swear you'd never gotten.) Rock lyrics convince us, without a direct word being said, that "If you're a virgin at age eighteen, you're either queer or a fool." No one on TV can be shown involved sexually unless they're *un*-married. The premise of most "reality" shows is that you *must* betray your comrades in order to "succeed." Holiness has a hard time even penetrating those almost universally accepted convictions. People in the 1950s, denied TV and CDs, thought completely otherwise. We *felt* the same urges; we just didn't *act* on them as readily as many do today. Why?

By far the majority of today's voices trying to sway our opinions are saying (without a direct word being said), "You'll achieve success as a human being if you can just accumulate enough money-fame-sex-power." I challenge anyone to deny that such propaganda has been overwhelmingly successful. But is that eminently effective propaganda *true?* Recall Elvis Presley, Marilyn Monroe, Kurt Cobain, River Phoenix, and the rest who had all that, in spades, but killed themselves. It's an undeniable objective fact that those things did not make them happy.

And yet a senior once told me he had spoken about his future the previous evening to his father, a graduate of Catholic grade school, college, and graduate school, now a stalwart of his parish and a daily communicant. The boy had said, "Dad, I've been given so much. I'd like to give something back. I'd like to be a teacher." And without taking a breath, the father said, "Now wait a minute! How the hell much can you make doing that?"

As Bertrand Russell said, "Many would rather die than think. Most of them do."

### Reductionism

All fair judgments about questions of doctrine or morality (or any decision) are jeopardized by resolutely resisting genuinely pertinent data. Prejudice blinds us to the objective fact that skin color or ethnicity or homeliness doesn't diminish a person's humanity. An unflinching ignorance of the evidence severely obstructs honest judgment, and most often makes the judge look like a fool. Vested interests put objective evidence into a perspective skewed out of kilter to the advantage of the arguer. Uncritical acceptance of what "everybody knows" sentenced Socrates to death, silenced Galileo, and nearly kept Columbus from sailing west.

*By far the majority of today's voices trying to sway our opinions are saying (without a direct word being said), "You'll achieve success as a human being if you can just accumulate enough money-fame-sex-power."*

We all want to be free. But, ironically, to be free *costs*. Genuine freedom requires the effort to gather, sift, outline, conclude, critique. But our animal inertia resists. Genuine freedom requires we accept *all* pertinent data, even facts that threaten the clarity (and consoling security) of our conclusions. Otherwise, all the actions we base on skewed conclusions will be at the very least inappropriate, at the very worst deadly to other people, and ultimately deadening to oneself.

In the end there is only one choice: be an authentically free human being or be a slave to your Id's snarling selfishness and your unexamined Superego's contradictory voices. And taped indelibly on that Superego, but still open to adult critique, are all the *religious* do's and don'ts about God, the soul, sin, and holiness we accepted indiscriminately as children. Most of those convictions we salted away during a period of religious education that, for the majority, ended just before we arrived at the use of our critical human faculties.

Contrary to all other modes in which we deal with the world now as adults, far too many of the best Christians still labor under the unexamined conviction that God has the same expectations for adults as for tractable children. On the contrary, although he intends us to be sheep in the hands of his Son, God intends us to be *shepherds* in regard to others.

## Jesus and Ambiguity

The servants asked him, "Do you want us to go and pull up the weeds?"

"No," he answered, "because while you are pulling the weeds, you may root up the wheat with them. Let both grow together until the harvest. At that time I will tell the harvesters: First collect the weeds and tie them in bundles to be burned; then gather the wheat and bring it into my barn." (Matt. 13:29–30)

My childhood playmates and I were filled with those inflexible certitudes one begins to harbor and harden from the age of about eight well into college. One little neighborhood girl had a truly unfortunate name, Catherine Isbister.

Worse in our Catholic eyes, she was a, well, a Protestant. One day (occasioned by who knows what) Catherine averred that babies came out of their mummies' tummies. Instinctively, atavistically, the rest of us little peanuts picked up small stones and threw them at Catherine! We were uncompromisingly certain this was some hellish Protestant heresy! Since then, I've formulated O'Malley's First Law: "The Less You Know, the More Certain You Can Be."

Oscar Hammerstein III put it about as succinctly as anyone:

> You've got to be taught before it's too late
> Before you are six or seven or eight
> To hate all the people your relatives hate
> You've got to be carefully taught.
>
> (*South Pacific*)

I haven't the slightest doubt Jesus would have taken no delight in our innocent cruelty. Nor could he have sanctioned the Inquisition, the bloody Crusades, the Huguenot persecution, the Salem witch hunts, the Holocaust, the McCarthy trials, or Jihad. His Father "causes his sun to rise on the evil and the good, and sends rain on the righteous and the unrighteous" (Matt. 5:45) and is content to leave such weighty and consequential judgments for a much later time.

Impartiality deals with scrupulous justice. But Jesus — and the whole fabric of Christianity — go incalculably *beyond* justice. They demand a love that yields to forgiveness, even *before* the malefactor has made amends. Consider carefully the details in the story of the prodigal son. The boy, suffering from his arrogant ways, comes to his senses and heads for home, memorizing his confession: "Father, I have sinned against heaven and against you. I am no longer worthy to be called your son; make me like one of your hired men" (Luke 15:18). When the runaway nears home, his father sees him "from afar off," implying he's out there every night, hoping. And the father runs to the boy, not the other way around. He throws his arms around him and kisses him *before* the kid has gotten out a single word of his confession! And he doesn't demand a list of the specific ways the boy wasted his patrimony nor does he give him a retributive penance. He gives him a *party!* The God of Jesus is well beyond the God of Justice.

Peter once asked Jesus if we have to forgive one another seven times. But Jesus gave the startling reply: "I tell you, not up to seven times, but seventy times seven!" (Matt. 18:22). That's 490 times! For each person! For each offense!

In *Les Misérables,* Victor Hugo shows the startling difference between justice and love. After nineteen years in the galleys for stealing one loaf of bread, Jean Valjean arrived in the town of Digne. Bishop Bienvenue welcomed him into his home after he'd been refused even the hospitality of the town jail, fed him at his own table, with the best dishes and silver, lit by silver candlesticks. That night, when everyone was asleep, Jean Valjean rose from his bed in the bishop's house, stole downstairs, and fled into the night with the bishop's silverware. Next morning, when the gendarmes brought Valjean in chains with the basket of silver to the bishop's door, Bishop Bienvenue said, "Ah, my friend! You forgot to take the silver candlesticks too!" And before the dumbfounded policemen, he handed the convict the candlesticks and closed the door with a smile. That was far beyond justice. Bishop Bienvenue was holy.

In *Dead Man Walking*, Sr. Helen Prejean totally accepted that outlandish belief too. When she was reviled for pleading for the life of Patrick Sonnier, a convicted murderer, she said, quite simply, "I'm just trying to do what I thought Jesus would do."

In the new Coventry Cathedral, destroyed by the Germans in World War II, they built an altar from the rubble, and into the splintered tabletop are burned two words, "Father, forgive."

When Gandhi was asked what he thought of Christianity, he reputedly replied, "I think it's perfectly marvelous. I just wish someone would try it."

What the chapter suggests is that we be more cautious in what we too readily believed as children and never updated and refined as adults. This talk of impartiality definitely does not mean that Jesus was a patsy and expected all good Christians to be pushovers too. If one stands for everything, one stands for nothing. Agnosticism is a perfectly admirable stance in the face of a serious dilemma. For a time. But those who insist on "keeping all the options open" will stand paralyzed for a lifetime at the first crossroads.

There is one indispensable requisite, for instance, for forgiveness: we have to take the first step and head for home. Unlike the hopes of so many, especially of the young, God does *not* "forgive everything, no matter what," simply because God will not force himself on anyone against their free will. We have to admit, honestly, our need for forgiveness. Then we have to swallow our arrogance and turn for home.

But we are getting way ahead of ourselves here. Love without self-reference and forgiveness for the undeserving are way down the line. First we have to reconsider our gratitude, our awareness of others, our respect, empathy, kindness, feeling of responsibility, and in general our overall susceptibility to being vulnerable rather than secure. But at least for the moment we have considered where the quest is headed. Till then, we content ourselves with examining on a far more basic level what obstacles within us might foreclose even the possibility of a human and then a divine connection.

*Agnosticism is a perfectly admirable stance in the face of a serious dilemma. For a time. But those who insist on "keeping all the options open" will stand paralyzed for a lifetime at the first crossroads.*

St. Ignatius Loyola proposes a very uncomplicated "Presupposition" before he will allow anyone to undertake or to direct his Spiritual Exercises:

> To assure better cooperation between the one who is giving the Exercises and the exercitant and more beneficial results to both, it is necessary to suppose that every good Christian is more ready to put a good interpretation on another's statement than to condemn it as false. If an

orthodox construction cannot be put on a proposition, the one who made it should be asked how he understands it. If he is in error he should be corrected with all kindness. If this does not suffice, all appropriate means should be used to bring him to a correct interpretation and so defend the proposition from error.

If we could inculcate that attitude in children's earliest years, if we could first show the ways in which all religions and moral systems are basically the same, if we could develop a tolerance for ambiguity rather than rushing to stake claims on the One True Religion, perhaps we might wipe out family feuds, gang turf wars, feminists vs. chauvinists, Hatfield-McCoy vendettas, liturgical bickering, border disputes, Thomists vs. Scotists, missionary conflicts with native religions, race riots, interfaith controversies, even worldwide wars and schisms. Maybe we could even eliminate controversies between liberals and conservatives.

It couldn't possibly be that easy. Could it?

## A Personal Examen

- Number each of the following issues in order of their importance to you personally. Cross out those which are relatively meaningless to you. Are there any that, frankly, infuriate you? Are any of your choices, honestly, motivated by (1) ingrained prejudice, (2) inadequate study of the alternatives, (3) vested interests, or (4) uncritical acceptance of false propaganda.

___ forest conservation

___ the world's hungry children

___ the plight of illegal immigrants

___ abortion

___ prayer in public schools

___ capital punishment

___ gun control

___ public school dropouts

___ terrorism

___ the aging and aged

___ materialist advertising

___ fewer number of priests

___ teenage pregnancies

___ wealthy control of government

___ ban on women priests

___ welfare cheats

___ dying cities

___ involvement in foreign wars

___ racial inequities

___ gay legal unions

- No one can crusade against many inequities, much less all of them, without going mad. But is there just one societal or ecclesiastical fault I could profitably dedicate some of my time and energy to?

- Psychologists claim that, while women will usually sit quietly, listening to understand where the speaker is coming from, males, especially boys, will start arguing long before they even know the speaker's thesis. Does that generalization stand up at least in part in my experience? If so, does it behoove me to reassess whether my righteous convictions ought to hold back a bit longer in arguments? Or does it suggest that I might be too reserved about my beliefs? A crucifix at least suggests Jesus did not intend Christians to be *too* reserved.

# Chapter Five

# Gratitude

*One of the [lepers], when he saw he was healed, came
back, praising God in a loud voice. He threw himself
at Jesus' feet and thanked him — and he was a Samaritan. Jesus asked, "Were not all ten cleansed? Where are
the other nine? Was no one found to return and give
praise to God except this foreigner?" Then he said to
him, "Rise and go; your faith has made you well."*

— Luke 17:15–19

SOME PEOPLE still remain contentedly self-shackled to the
humans-only potential to ask why. This, despite all formal schooling has done to smother that curious urge with
academic certitudes. One impasse that is particularly troublesome is the seeming contradiction in those who on the one
hand profess a belief in God, and on the other find no need
to worship. Quite unlikely anyone who has read this far fits
that dilemma, but surely your soul is troubled by people you
love for whom it is true.

The Bible offers no definition of God, but he is clearly the
ultimate Creator and Sustainer, the One who called each of
us (as e. e. cummings put it) "from the no of all nothing."

The Good Book does allude to this personage's attributes. He is Spirit (John 4:24), infinitely powerful (Dan. 4:35), absolutely wise and truthful (Heb. 6:18), utterly holy (Lev. 11:44). He reveals himself and his will through the inward natures of all he made (Rom. 1:20) and through his Son (Heb. 1:1–2). No matter what names and specifications we apply to him, there is only one true God (Deut. 6:4), eternal, transcendent, existing before, apart from, and independently of anything made.

This personage sounds quite frightfully important: the One without whom I would not exist. And on that single initial gift of existence depends everything else that I know and love.

Puzzling that someone could accept a Being so integral to one's life, yet not feel *consumed* by a need to express one's indebtedness, again and again and again.

*Nobility comes from recognizing, with honest gratitude, that one has been blessed and is therefore obligated, in honor, to be generous to the less fortunate.*

Say, for instance, a zillionaire pulled up next to you in his Rolls-Royce, opened the window, and said, "You look like a promising sort. Here's a certified check for a million dollars. Have a good day." Up goes the window, and off he drives.

If the stupefied recipient didn't even try to discover who that guy was, and where he lived, and how to thank him, breathlessly, over and over, he or she would be one mean-spirited S.O.B. (Sorry, there's no better designation for such an unconscionable ingrate.)

And if this God opened the door to *everything*. . . .

Yet ingratitude seems to be one of the major gifts bequeathed to us by Adam and Eve. The best of parents (who didn't really *have* to have children in the first place) spend twenty-five years or more of their one life raising, feeding, protecting, puzzling over, worrying about children so that they will develop such independence that one day they can come and say, "Mom and Dad, I've found someone I love more than I love you two — or at least in a much different way. Bye!"

On the contrary, parents who (even wordlessly) *expect* gratitude seem bad parents. "Don't ever forget you have me to thank for that. . . . No, no! I gave you my whole life, but don't mention it. . . . You go ahead and have fun. There's sure to be a good rerun of *The Simpsons.*"

As the King of Siam said, "Is a puzzlement."

## Noblesse Oblige

Bees sip honey from flowers and hum their thanks when
　　they leave.
The gaudy butterfly is sure that the flowers owe thanks
　　to him.　　　　　　　　　　(Rabindranath Tagore)

Probably not too many dukes or duchesses (even minor ones) will read these pages, but those words, "Nobility obligates," are true for all of us. Real nobility has nothing to do with bloodlines and the right to inherit despite one's embarrassing limitations. It denotes a solidity of character or spirit that scorns whatever is petty, mean, or dishonorable. Nobility comes from recognizing, with honest gratitude, that one has been blessed and is therefore obligated, in honor, to be generous to the less fortunate.

The profoundest obstacle to honest gratitude is refusal to accept the fact one *is,* indeed, gifted beyond imagining! Many (perhaps most) take our giftedness for granted, as if they were somehow "entitled." Again, anyone interested in a book like this quite likely doesn't qualify on that score. On the other hand, they could be just as deluded about their worth because of a satanic humility. They refuse to admit their blessedness, in wrongful self-abasement and horror of arrogance. "Oh, I'm nobody. Really." What an insult to the Giver of Life!

No matter under which motive we deny our fantastic blessedness, it's no wonder so many find it difficult to feel grateful. The humble Mother of God understood the liberating truth:

> My soul glorifies the Lord
> and my spirit rejoices in God my Savior,
> for he has been mindful
> of the humble state of his servant.
> From now on, all generations will call me blessed,
> for the Mighty One has done great things for me —
> holy is his name.          (Luke 1:46–49)

Before continuing, it would be wise to draw some distinctions that many even well-schooled adults don't make between "guilt" and "responsibility." Although it is invisible and can be denied, guilt is real, a fact that comes into existence when someone is culpable for some real offense, when one knows he or she is incontestably responsible for a bad result. I did, in fact, fail to get that job done. But the *fact* of the guilt (and resultant responsibility to do something about it) is quite different from *accepting* both. Being the responsible party and acting the responsible person are two different things. In my experience too many people groan "Guilt trip!" when put on the spot about their moral (human) behavior, not because the suggestion is unfair, but because it *is* fair, and they don't want to admit that or submit to the ways they would have to change if they did admit it.

*Just as hunger in the belly leads us to keep ourselves alive, genuine guilt is a hunger that says I'm not really okay at the moment, and I ought to do something about it to become a more fulfilled human person.*

Being self-absorbed is part of our inheritance from our ape ancestors. But the human invitation is to rise above animal narcissism and open ourselves to broader and richer horizons. We can transcend our animal nature, but it's not going to go away. That self-absorption makes me want to feel okay about myself — all the time, even at times when I don't have a real *right* to feel okay. Therefore, when someone gets inside my defenses and upsets my comfy equilibrium with a suggestion that (1) I've done something wrong and (2) I ought to do something about it, the animal in me bristles, sneers, tries to bat it away.

Of course guilt trips can be psychologically destructive, but only when the cause of the guilt is either unmerited or out of proportion. Dropping a pass, for instance, is embarrassing but in the first place, the intended receiver didn't *plan* to bobble it, and in the second place, the violation is hardly in a league with gassing six million Jews or even a single murder or even the casual assassination of someone's reputation. (Absolutely nothing to do with "sin" or religion here; just whether we have an honest right to feel good about ourselves. Religion adds to that thoughtlessness a failure to appreciate not just one's gifts but the Giver.)

Contrary to what many would like to believe, honest guilt is a very salutary reality. Just as hunger in the belly leads us to keep ourselves alive, genuine guilt is a hunger that says I'm not really okay at the moment, and I ought to do something about it to become a more fulfilled human person. The first step is honestly to judge whether I am, in fact, responsible for some misguided act, then hold myself accountable for it, then take steps to rectify it, no matter how much effort or embarrassment it means. To take the first step without the second is deadly: sort of half-heartedly admitting I've done something wrong, then carrying around the unfocused guilt like a toothache I'd like to forget. Unless genuine guilt becomes genuine responsibility, it is useless. Or worse, it corrodes the

entire self from the inside. That is why the Sacrament of Reconciliation is an inestimable gift: shedding oneself of guilt,
definitively, actually *hearing* the forgiveness.

Therefore, in what follows regarding our giftedness and its
natural connection with our sense of gratitude for it, there
is no intention to make anyone guilty about being gifted. In
most cases like looks, economic status, family background,
and so forth, you are not responsible; someone else gave them
to you. The question is rather what you've made of your gifts,
like the servant in the parable, entrusted talents by the master.
Other than taxes, no external law says Oprah Winfrey has to
share with the less fortunate the abundance she achieved out
of what she was given. The "law" is inside Oprah. It's what
ennobles her as a human being.

Sometimes you hear about a "self-made" man or woman.
No one is self-made. Each of us stands on the shoulders of
countless others. Oprah honestly credits her no-nonsense father and stepmother, her teachers, even her own neglectful
mother, for her success. Without her own indestructible spirit,
of course, she never would have become what she became.
But without those other people, she never would have done
it either.

If you can read this page, you are gifted. Nearly a third
of the citizens of this gifted country are functionally illiterate, able to read street signs and brand names but completely
incapable of reading the directions on a cake-mix box or de-
ciphering a map. Someone (do you remember who?) taught
you how to read, and other people challenged you to read
more and more complex writing, year after year. How many

of us ever thought to thank them for such an inestimable gift? "Oh, well, they had to do it. That's what they got paid for." Nope. They could have had a lot fewer hassles and made a lot more money working in a napalm factory.

Public service ads remind us of bloat-bellied children in Africa, displaced families, and refugees, in an attempt to elicit funds to help them. They are, knowingly or not, playing on our guilt/responsibility. What they fail to do, I believe, is take the earlier step of simply reminding each of us how lucky we are. Most of us look around a group like an office or party and rarely focus on the people dressed more poorly than we are; it's usually the ones who are better off, so that envy takes the place of gratitude. And yet the materially poorest person in those rooms is overwhelmingly better off than the majority of people with whom we share this planet. No guilt involved in that; it's no one's fault we were born here rather than there, or that our parents were able to achieve more materially than most of the world's parents. Not guilt but a sense of giftedness, of gratitude.

Whenever someone asks me, "How ya doin'?" I usually say, "Probably better than I deserve." They, in turn, almost always say, "Well, of course you deserve...." What? I didn't deserve to be born! I didn't exist. How could a nonbeing *deserve* anything? Granted that if I'd never existed I'd never have known the difference. But I *do* exist. If I tried to write out all the things and people I love, that give me joy, enrich my life, it would take me years! Yet why do so many of us waste so much time moaning about what we haven't got and completely ignore all we have. Oprah says: "Don't complain about what you don't have. Use what you've got." If Cinderella complained she had to leave the ball at midnight, the Fairy Godmother might well have said, "Sweetie, who said you could even come to the ball in the first place?"

---

*Someone (do you remember who?) taught you how to read, and other people challenged you to read more and more complex writing, year after year. How many of us ever thought to thank them for such an inestimable gift?*

---

The Lebanese writer Kahlil Gibran wrote that if your task is to make a chair, make it as if your beloved were to use it. If gratitude and love are genuine, and not merely comforting lies we tell ourselves and believe, there is no honest possibility of settling for half-hearted endurance of boredom, cutting corners, playing the odds, testing the limits of others' patience. Could anyone play those underhanded games with people they claim truly to *love?*

## The Eucharist

Well, toward morning the conversation turned on the Eucharist, which I, being the Catholic, was obviously supposed to defend. Mrs. Broadwater [the author, Mary McCarthy] said when she was a child and received the Host, she thought of it as the Holy Ghost, He being the "most portable" person of the Trinity; now she thought of it as a symbol and implied that it was a pretty good one. I then said, in a very shaky voice, "Well, if it's a symbol, to hell with it."                    (Flannery O'Connor)

The word "Eucharist" means thanksgiving. And to appreciate that, one must be humble enough to accept how stunningly blessed and privileged each of us is.

The true question is not what is the Eucharist, but who is the Eucharist. The *Catechism* says:

- We must therefore consider the Eucharist as: thanksgiving and praise to the Father; the sacrificial memorial of Christ and his Body, the presence of Christ by the power of his word and of his Spirit. (1358)

- In the Eucharistic sacrifice the whole of creation loved by God is presented to the Father through the death and the resurrection of Christ. Through Christ the Church can offer the sacrifice of praise in thanksgiving for all that God has made good, beautiful, and just in creation and in humanity. (1359)

- In the Eucharist Christ gives us the very body which he gave up for us on the cross, the very blood which he "poured out for many for the forgiveness of sins." (1365)

Three of the four Gospels and St. Paul record the initiation of the Holy Eucharist in substantially the same words:

While they were eating, Jesus took bread, gave thanks and broke it, and gave it to his disciples, saying, "Take and eat; this is my body." Then he took the cup, gave thanks and offered it to them, saying, "Drink from it, all of you. This is my blood of the covenant, which is poured out for many for the forgiveness of sins." (Matt. 26:25–29; see also Mark 14:22–25; Luke 22:19–23; 1 Cor. 11:23–25)

In none of the accounts does Jesus say, or even imply, that this is merely symbolic, like a reenactment of a Civil War battle or a remembrance like a birthday. "This *is* my body. . . . This *is* my blood." And although the fourth Gospel has no description of the event, Jesus does underline his literal intentions in a way only a fanatic could question: "Unless you eat the flesh of the Son of Man and drink His blood you will not have life in you" (John 6:53). In John 6:47–67 Jesus refuses to soften those words about the nature of his presence in the bread and wine, even when so many refused to stay with him because of them. Had he meant only that the bread and wine would "signify" him, he could easily have made that clear, and no one would have left.

Our senses perceive surfaces, accidents; only the mind can attempt to grasp the substance. My estimates of others from their looks are quite often wildly erroneous. Without our awareness, everyone in North America is, at this very moment, speeding eastward at 750 mph. The rock that split the skin of my knee only *appears* flinty but is actually aswarm with galaxy upon galaxy of whizzing particles. All day long we are pierced by neutrinos, which have virtually no mass, no electric charge, and move through the whole earth without being significantly slowed down. Most of the reality in this room is real but inaccessible to my senses. No! *Yes!*

How could Jesus, the Eternal Son of God, squeeze himself into little wafers of bread and a cup of ordinary wine? The same way he could diminish himself into an infant in a manger. And, to speak in the same vein as Flannery O'Connor, the God who found no difficulty making a universe out of nothing can do whatever he damn well pleases.

There is a further aspect of the Eucharist that some are reluctant to consider:

> Is not the cup of thanksgiving for which we give thanks a participation in the blood of Christ? And is not the bread that we break a participation in the body of Christ? Because there is one loaf, we, who are many, are one body, for we all partake of the one loaf. (1 Cor. 10:16–17)

The solitary Christian is a contradiction. "By this all men will know that you are my disciples, if you love one another" (John 13:35). Simple, and difficult, as that. (Just be grateful Jesus didn't say "like"!) No matter what we might think of our fellow passengers in the Barque of Peter, we are all in this together, and the Mass at least ought to be a reminder of that.

In the years since Vatican Council II, liturgical scholars have wrought many changes in the fabric of Eucharistic celebration, some slowly, some jarringly sudden for old-timers. There is a whole different "feel" to it for them. Even the old-shoe comfort of the word "Mass" yielded to the more academic-sounding "liturgy." To put the change too simply, the major focus has been shifted from awesome regard for the Host at the center of the meal out to the enlivening that should take place within the participating community. Just as in the mystery of the Incarnation, the awesome Ancient of Days from the books of Daniel and Isaiah and Revelation has come down from his fiery throne and settled into the manger of Bethlehem, the Nazareth carpenter's shop, and the Upper Room of the first Eucharistic meal. The priest no longer stands like a lens between the altar and congregation, mediating between the two. Rather the table is at the center, as with any other family meal. The tabernacle is no longer the core of attention, as it was, and there are some theologians not quite sure Christ is really as energetically present locked up in a box as he is in the dynamic workings of the Eucharist-in-progress. New church buildings are now less like gloomy, awesome halls and more like the airy lounges of a spa or ski resort. The whole attitude is more "homey" and less "forbidding."

All well and good, but, to continue being completely honest, something has been lost in the trade-off for those whose faith is more a matter of a heart-to-heart friendship than a theological enterprise. And successful enactment of the Eucharist depends much more on the skills of the ministers than it once did. A well-intentioned young man in a cardigan with a guitar is no substitute for the swell of an organ. The reluctant mewing of an unprepared audience hardly stimulates the soul. Many participants, trained to be more reserved, actually find the handshake at the Greeting of Peace more repellent than unitive. Far more expectations now rest on the accomplishments of the homilist than before. If that happens to be true for any Catholic, then it is incumbent on him or her to *find* a parish whose liturgy meets their soul needs and do a lot of serious strengthening of their personal faith.

For centuries, the statues and stained glass were "the illiterate's Bible," supports for a peasant faith that faced fewer alternatives and doubts than we do today. The poorest churches impoverished themselves for an organ to bear up on its broad shoulders the congregation's untrained voices. Even the unintelligible Latin lent the occasion an intriguing mystique. Now, just as in the bare cave of Bethlehem and on the weedy shore of the Lake of Tiberias, it requires a firmer faith to discover the omnipotent God within the ordinary and unimposing.

To remain perfectly honest, if the manner of worship available is unsatisfying — because it's "too high-Church and hoity-toity" or because it's "too commonplace and threadbare" — those who remain engrafted in the visible Church despite their discomfort are proof of the real meaning of worship. As foolish and unfeeling to ask them why they remain as to ask a couple married fifty years why they've stayed together so long. If you have to ask, you simply couldn't understand.

When kids tell me they don't go to Mass anymore "because I don't get anything out of it," my ready answer is, "Of course not, silly! Because that's not what it's for!"

## A Personal Examen

- Who taught me to read? Was there someone during my adolescence who treated me other than like an alien mutant? Who first gave me a sense that I might just have something to offer the world? Who helped ease the way at my first job? Are they still living? Where could I look for an address?

- At the very outset of his book, in the midst of his awesome torments, Job's wife tells him, "Curse God and die!" But he answers, "Shall we accept good from God, and not trouble?" Only then do his so-called comforters arrive who, in their uncritical orthodoxy, insist he must have done something to deserve his anguish since God doesn't inflict suffering without reason. They completely skew the issue into a matter of *justice* rather than a question of *faith* between friends. Do I ever pause and reflect, "Hey! I don't have a cold today! Wow! Isn't it great that I don't have a headache!" Do I have an unwitting gut feeling there should be no negatives in a "fair" world?

- What are the moments in my life that seemed — and at the time *were* in my eyes — unbearable assaults by God on my faith and serenity, which I thought I could never forgive, and yet which paradoxically turned out to be "blessings in disguise"? Do I remind myself of that often enough?

- Let me look around "my living space" at all the specially collected "stuff." What are the specific things among my possessions that I simply take for granted but that nine-tenths of the world's inhabitants can only dream of? Does it suggest anything about the kind of attitude I ought to have toward what I have? Does it make it more difficult to feel sorry for myself?

• Let me put the book aside awhile and allow the faces of those I truly love to unfold in my imagination, like a slow-motion film, lingering on one face until another eases into its place. Aren't they even more precious *because* I didn't deserve them?

# Chapter Six

# Awareness

*You have heard it said, "Eye for eye, and tooth for tooth." But I tell you, Do not resist an evil person. If someone strikes you on the right cheek, turn to him the other also. And if someone wants to sue you and take your tunic, let him have your cloak as well. If someone forces you to go one mile, go with him two miles. Give to the one who asks you, and do not turn away from the one who wants to borrow from you.*

*— Matthew 5:38–42*

As we saw before, several light years stretch between that admirably altruistic ideal in the Sermon on the Mount and the soul-place where most of us feel impelled to say, "Thus far. No further!" The territorial growls of the Beast in us are not silenced by baptism, nor by a lifetime of sincere resolutions. The sting from the last slap on the cheek often still burns so fiercely that we unreflectively "decide" never again to be hurt like that. As a result, we desensitize our radars and raise our protective force-fields so we needn't even notice most of the people we brush past all day, who might intrude on our security. Settle in with a few comfortable tested and trusted friends and family, and mind your own business. "Good fences make good neighbors."

In an epically overstimulated society like our own, that defensiveness is completely understandable. If we left all our sensors wide open, they'd be burned out in a few minutes! The question is: Have we perhaps *over*-compensated? Have we settled for what Susan Sontag called "saving indifference"? Just as our society and Church were once scrupulously watchful about the slightest sexual innuendo, to the point of prudery and suppression of the Id rather than domesticating its power, is it possible some of us have become so sensitive to the slightest threat to our tranquility that we not only deny life-giving friendships but, unwittingly, wall out the majority of those to whom Christ missions us?

Awhile ago I read a newspaper piece about a fifteen-year-old boy arrested for the brutal murder of an old woman for a few dollars. They asked if he felt any remorse. "She's not me," he answered. "Why should I care about her?" To anyone who reads the papers, that attitude is not unique. Such sociopaths, only a few steps beyond the animal, are totally self-absorbed. The only real person in the world is myself, exactly like Helen Keller before her liberation. The others are only incomprehensible objects that bump against me in the dark.

In his native African hospital, Dr. Albert Schweitzer said that, whenever he asked an ambulatory patient to give a bedridden patient a drink of water, the native might say, "This man is not brother of me." An only slightly larger scope of awareness than total self-centeredness, concern for those of my tribe but no further. Yet even in a society as brutal as our own, defensively desensitized as we are against so much inhumanity, any civilized person would at least wince at an egomania that limits awareness and concern to one's own "tribe" or, more tragically, to oneself alone.

---

*Unfortunately caution too often outweighs venturesomeness so that, even when we reach adulthood, we have to be reminded that humanity invites us beyond the cocoon, and Jesus invites us far further than that. He didn't say, "The cautious shall inherit the earth."*

---

It is the primary task of parents and teachers to civilize that self-absorbed Beast in us, not only by imposing limits on a child's rambunctiousness but also by widening the child's radius of awareness of, and then concern for, persons living beyond the tight inner circles of "me and mine."

Yet we can find no basis for that respect and concern for others in the biological world. Awareness, yes, but always rigid with distrust. One life form preserves itself by destroying others. The series of fish, each larger than the last, readying to devour the one in front has become a cliché for the corporate jungle of monopoly capitalism. The jaguar stalks the gazelle, the wolf falls upon the lamb, even the perky robin hauls up the hapless worm with its beak, as indifferent as the boy who murdered the old woman.

The boy-murderer *is* a human being — like the pimp, the pusher, the terrorist — but his human potential has never been activated. He is just over the line from the wolf, most likely destined to stay there. Humans are born with a *capacity* to be better than beasts because we can reason, but neither reasoning nor acting humanly are mandatory, the way rapacity in a beast is irresistible. We are free to ignore our reasoning capacity and our humanity, even to pervert them. That self-protectiveness does, indeed, keep us from walking unlighted streets, and even if we do become sensitized to the enrichment of reaching beyond our limits, we don't leave that gut wariness behind. The most basic, and paradoxical, responsibility of parents is to make their children feel safe, but *without* smothering their human impulse to crawl beyond the blanket. They are stunted unless they become more and more aware of the web of human relationships that stretches beyond the limits of their own skins — to their families, then beyond family to work and community, beyond community to the nation, and beyond that to the whole human family.

In the parable of the Good Samaritan, the radical fault in the God-fearing priest and the pious Levite was not their lack of charity but their apparently habitual skill in distracting their attention from the troublesome presence of the beaten man intruding on their serenity. The precondition of the Samaritan's kindness was allowing himself to notice the victim was even there.

Unfortunately caution too often outweighs venturesomeness so that, even when we reach adulthood, we have to be reminded that humanity invites us beyond the cocoon, and

Jesus invites us far further than that. He didn't say, "The cautious shall inherit the earth."

## A Sense of Others

For the first years of our infancy, we were little different from healthy little animals — eating, excreting, exploring: "doin' what comes natcherly." All reality was merely an extension of ourselves, completely self-absorbed. But with what seems supernatural patience, good parents work night and day to develop in us a humans-only reciprocity, mutuality. At first an uncritically accepted series of no-no's, then (hopefully) a felt sense of our separateness from others — without erasing a sense of community with them. "They have feelings, too."

That hardly seems an insight worth stressing with adults in a book like this. Yet, as we have seen, in total honesty all but the certified saints among us have to admit there are some "types" about whom we find it difficult to sense that "they have feelings too." In playing the game of "Trust," falling back and letting someone else catch you, even a lifelong friend will look behind and say with an uneasy grin, "You're not gonna pull anything, right?"

With genuine wisdom, parents tell children, "Do *not* talk to strangers!" But at what age does that advice become not only as useless but as inhibiting as "Be seen and not heard"? Are there some who still uncritically accept that admonition well into adulthood as an unchallenged requirement for what they wrongly believe is self-preservation?

Think a moment of your very best friends. At one time, *they* were strangers. What was the absolutely first thing you had to do in order to make a heart-to-heart friendship even remotely possible? Not introducing yourself. Not exchanging names. Even before those, the *sine qua non* step was to *notice* them, to fixate that face and form out of the madding crowd, make the primary effort to individualize this one person from the six and a half billion others, by far the majority of whom you will never even be aware of. Without that notice, nothing. Then in the normal order of things we attach a name and perhaps a few incidental details that make the person an acquaintance. "Oh, yeah, I know who she is." When you think of it, almost all the people you claim to know remain acquaintances.

In any given weekday, especially in larger cities, we brush past literally thousands of people without so much as a single click of awareness. If we need an ATM, that is the only configuration that emerges from the smear of stimuli. Test yourself sometime during a regular move, say, down your street or a corridor in your office or school. Just for the fun of it, try to count the number of faces you pass in those few minutes that you have never "seen" before, even though most of them simply couldn't be newcomers. Then if you can muster the *chutzpah,* bring yourself to say a simple, "Hi!" to whoever is brave enough to catch eyes. Some are even audacious enough to speak to others waiting for the same delayed flight, in the laundromat, or even in an elevator! If it becomes a habit, I suspect your day will be a lot more cheerful, and it's quite likely either you or the other person will say, "Are you going for coffee too?" It sounds so stupidly simple!

"Friends" are people you don't mind sitting with at lunch; "pals" are the ones you *expect* to sit with. Most of those moves from acquaintances to friends just sort of "happen": same patterns, similar interests, and a real-but-tenuous bond forms. They attach themselves, and you just don't brush them off. You share time and talk, during which two parallel but real connections take place. On the surface, chit-chat that's hardly worth chipping into marble; beneath that, a wordless "I enjoy being with you." That sure beats eating alone!

With pals, you've shared some more serious mutual burden: the martinet manager, a natural disaster, a wake, the same team or privet hedge. Again, this stronger bonding usually happens without an intention, but more importantly without any sheepish resistance either.

Best friends happen, as one student put it, "when you cry together." The helpless need is so powerful, you collapse *all* the defenses. You allow the other behind the bravado with which the Wizard of Oz protects himself, invite him or her behind the impressive tapestry to become aware of all the snarls and knots. We "give ourselves away." And the other says, "So what? We're still friends." If you are gifted with such friends, grapple them to your heart with hoops of steel. There is no greater treasure.

You can have as many people inside that precious innermost circle as you choose. But — and that's a prodigious "but" — at each of those progressive stages sits a doorway, and it has only one handle, on the inside. Each one involves an act of faith, a moment of vulnerability, which depends on your confidence in yourself and your belief that nine times out of ten, when you trust others, your trust is justified. For many, the risk just seems too great, and rather than risk that one admittedly painful betrayal, they will forego those nine friendships. Sad, really.

> *Best friends happen, as one student put it, "when you cry together."*

"Do not forget to entertain strangers, for by so doing some people have entertained angels without knowing it" (Heb. 13:2). Imagine: snubbing an angel from fear of "getting involved."

And the Kingdom of God suffers as well. The Founder's intentions are subverted. "I came so they can have real and eternal life, more and better life than they ever dreamed of" (John 10:10).

## A Personal Examen

- In the early 1940s, in a startling number of camps around Europe, men and women of the German SS ordered and assisted in the systematic extermination of six million Jews and eleven million Gentiles, either by direct gassing or by slow starvation and overwork. A great many of them had no personal grudge against their victims; they were just doing a job, "following orders." What's more, they were people who would never even think of kicking their neighbor's dog. Some of them spent the work day routinely exterminating human beings (many of them children) and then went home to play Mozart on the piano. What got lost?

• Make a list of sketchy descriptions of at least five people you live or work with, for example, the one by the window with the tacky blonde hair, lipstick too brassy, etc. Leave room at the side of the list to write their names when you discover them. Then make some kind of mark when you've introduced yourself, and another then you've had a five-minute conversation. Even that beats nothing.

• One time in a subway car, a scraggly, unshaven man sat, glassy-eyed, shouting curses at the other passengers safely hidden behind their newspapers. From out of the press of bodies emerged a young woman, plain-looking, almost mousy. She sat next to the raving man and took his hand in both her hands. She told him her name very quietly. The man looked as shocked as the rest of us. His shoulders sank; his voice softened. And they sat peacefully together, her soft voice soothing him. What did she have that I surely don't?

• "Here's another way to put it: You're here to be light, bringing out the God-colors in the world. God is not a secret to be kept. We're going public with this, as public as a city on a hill. If I make you light-bearers, you don't think I'm going to hide you under a bucket, do you? I'm putting you on a light stand. Now that I've put you there on a hilltop, on a light stand — shine! Keep open house; be generous with your lives. By opening up to

others, you'll prompt people to open up with God, this
generous Father in heaven" (Matt. 5:14–16). Are there
any obstacles between my soul and that admonition
from Jesus?

# Chapter Seven

# Empathy

*Then the righteous will answer him, "Lord, when did
we see you hungry and feed you, or thirsty and give you
something to drink?"* —Matthew 25:37

PERHAPS IT IS NO MORE than semantic nicety but, even
though the root meaning of all three words is exactly
the same, in everyday usage "compassion" and "sympathy"
seem to me more a matter of "feeling *for*," and "empathy"
means "feeling *with*," the first two being a bestowal (my heart
is moved to pity, from outside) and the other being mutual
ownership of suffering (I share the anguish, inside). The cause
is probably a science fiction film I saw and forget, except
that some characters were "Empaths," who literally underwent the same pains as the victims they focused their powers
upon. I feel the same difference as between "judgment" and
"kinship."

Every year when we ponder in class what being part of a
family means, I show Robert Redford's film *Ordinary People*.
I've seen it now probably thirty times, but every time I switch
off the tape at the end, after the son has finally been able
to tell his father he loves him, and the father tells the boy

he loves him too, I end up with tears in my eyes. One year, I mentioned that, and from the class (all boys) came mock groans and hoots of "Awww!" Apparently, to feel deeply for a stranger, or at least to admit it, is very "uncool."

I pulled myself up to my inconsiderable height and glared. "You guys really *scare* me, you know that?" They sobered up pretty fast. "Are your defenses so strong you can't even allow yourself at least a bit of fellow-feeling for a man and boy whose wife and mother just walked out on them because she was afraid of being vulnerable, and they just cling together in shared pain?"

*By the time little kids reach kindergarten, they've seen more deaths, real or fictional, than a lifetime veteran in the army of Genghis Khan, to the point psychiatrists say they can't tell the difference between real pain and acted pain.*

I wondered aloud, in genuine apprehension, how they would ever learn to open their innermost selves to their wives or respond when an unmarried daughter announced she was pregnant. These were, after all, boys who moaned that they had suffered eleven years of "Catholic brainwashing"! Had no one ever posed for them the crux of the only question of the Last Judgment, which determined if their whole lives had any value: their *compassion?* Had no one, in all those years, proposed to them the scandal of the crucifix? And in their last year in a Catholic school, for most of them their last time being pushed to consider that life-norm, how could I even try to "save" them from lifelong atrophy of the soul?

One kid sneered, "Well, you can feel sorry for somebody without breaking down into sobs." My guess was he exaggerated my reaction so he could reduce it to something absurd, and therefore not have to censor his own callousness in any way. Besides, just like "Don't talk to strangers," "Real boys don't cry" had taken far firmer root in him than "I tell you the truth, whatever you did not do for one of the least of these, you did not do for me" (Matt. 25:45).

This general "soul-numbing" is, again, understandable. By the time little kids reach kindergarten, they've seen more deaths, real or fictional, than a lifetime veteran in the army of Genghis Khan, to the point psychiatrists say they can't tell the difference between real pain and acted pain. Not only films but video games bristle with explosions and mayhem until those scenes are no longer able to move — or even shock. On the other hand, we're also besieged with public service announcements showing African children with great glistening eyes and flies drinking their tears, making anyone soul-bruised to the point it becomes just too much. We flick the dial, turn the page, become amnesiac. Muzzle our humanity.

Understandable, but as we saw in the last chapter, also impoverishing. At the core of *Ordinary People* is the need of the mother, Beth, and the son, Conrad, to have "control." The elder brother, Buck, had died in a boating accident. At Buck's funeral, Beth and Conrad were the only ones who didn't cry.

They couldn't risk what grieving would have cost them. And Conrad felt such inexpressible guilt at having survived the accident that he had tried to cut his wrists. The father, Calvin, reaches out to both of them, but they can't allow him access to their pain, nor can they allow themselves to identify with his pain. But as Burger, the psychiatrist in the film, says, "If you can't feel pain [your own or another's], you're not going to be able to feel anything else." The cocoon may very well be protective, but it is also very cramped and smothering.

In a very real sense, the words "empathy," "sympathy," and "compassion" are all "victim" words, and since — the crucifix, perhaps, notwithstanding — few of us have been encouraged to admire victims (only to pity them), even the words are scary to consider. They all go far beyond what my uneasy student meant by "feel sorry for," a pity that can be very remote, cool, only slightly warmer then indifference. It also goes beyond respect, which we can honestly offer another without any personal entanglement or cost. Respect is the first step on the road to justice; empathy is the first step on the road to love. Kindness is a step between the two.

## Kindness

In another classic, Harper Lee's *To Kill a Mockingbird,* the wise Atticus Finch tells his daughter, Scout,

> If you can learn a simple trick, Scout, you'll get along a lot better with all kinds of folks. You never really understand a person until you consider things from his

point of view — until you climb into his skin and walk around in it.

Take the case of the panhandler. Everyone reading this page has probably been ambushed by at least a few. The standard, practical response, as with the reverend priest and pious Levite in the parable of the Good Samaritan, is: divert your attention and pass by on the other side of the road. The indigent are almost certainly going to squander whatever you give on booze or drugs, right? Especially if they're disheveled and smell bad. You can almost convince yourself you're doing them a *kindness* by denying them help. But remember the wise Atticus. How did this person get where he is right now? Quite likely he wasn't always this way. Would anyone really choose to surrender his dignity, his self-esteem, to put out his paw and beg from strangers? And, looking from the broader perspective, what's he asking for? Far less than the cost of a candy bar. (You can see why gratitude came first in these pages.)

If you sincerely want to be a caring person, and you're honestly afraid the beggar will use your gift to harm himself, buy him a sandwich or a banana. If (as can happen) he sneers at your naivete and really is a phony, you'll have proven to yourself that *you* are not. The question here is not whether the beggar is in authentic need but whether you are authentically kind. Compassion goes as far as the heart; kindness gets into the hands.

Just as I'm willing to take the risk of one soul-bruising rather than chance losing nine potential friends, I'd rather be bilked by nine beggars than pass by the tenth in genuine need. And if you give a gift certificate at Christmas, you don't say, "Now you be sure to use that for something I'd approve of." Is it a gift or not?

Charity and courtesy can be faked; kindness can't. Witness the natural motherly ease in two famous and utterly different women who died the same week in September 1997, Princess Diana of Wales and Mother Teresa of Calcutta, caressing hurt children, whose wise eyes showed awed acceptance of such vulnerable kindness. When someone is "there" for you, it's not like a 911 number you can use if you're humble enough. It means they feel your pain and, even though they can't "solve" your suffering, they reach out to assure you that you're not alone. At a wake, for instance, nothing anyone can say will make the pain go away. All friends can do is put their arms around you and "say," wordlessly, "I don't know the answer either, but you're not alone."

But some families, even today, are very ill at ease with touch. Physical vulnerability seems (by nature, perhaps, but surely by nurture) more acceptable for girls than for boys — except in the clash of bodies when one has scored a goal. Too many parents, even today, fret unless little girls play with dolls and little boys never cry, never show tenderness, and surely never, ever touch anyone except with clear sexual goals. There also seems an unwritten societal law (at least in societies perverted by the Anglo-Saxon, Calvinist ethos) that when boys gets into the later years of grade school, fathers have to stop touching them, and both seem to submit wordlessly to that ukase. Again, okay to roughhouse, but not to caress.

The women's movement has made admirable strides in convincing males that the sexual stereotypes are not only insulting to women but also psychologically impoverishing to men. More men nowadays share tasks more simple-minded ages restricted to females (and slaves). But I can testify from forty-five years' teaching adolescent boys that too many believe that males who off-handedly touch one another are homosexual. That's a tragic limitation on the meaning of "love."

*If you never allow yourself to be taken in, you'll never see the inside of anything.*

In Kurt Vonnegut's novel *God Bless You, Mr. Rosewater,* a woman asks a gentle, generous eccentric to give her child a commandment to live by, and he says, "There's only one commandment: Goddammit, you've got to be kind."

### Loving

We all want to love and be loved, or at least we claim we do. But if we genuinely want a goal, there ought to be sufficient concrete evidence in our everyday lives to "convict" us of that. If we claim to be loving persons, we should be unable to escape that accusation simply because of our practical, habitual behavior and responses. In order for true loving to have even a chance, we have first to give the other our awareness, only then our respect, our empathy and kindness. Real loving costs. If it doesn't, using the word "love" is a delusion.

"If you love those who love you, what credit is that to you? Even sinners love those who love them" (Luke 6:32). We can be stingy with our loving, restricting its scope to a very narrow, insulated group. If what makes humans different from other animals is that we can *keep* learning and loving, then the more we learn and love, the more our lives, our selves, are enriched. The only obstacle to that enrichment is our own fear of being "taken in," hoaxed, made to look foolish. But if you never allow yourself to be taken in, you'll never see the inside of anything.

Jesus dares us to go even further. "He answered: 'Love the Lord your God with all your heart and with all your soul and with all your strength and with all your mind, and love your neighbor as yourself' " (Luke 10:27).

Remember, he didn't say "like." What he evidently did say, though, is "the same way you love yourself," which is almost as insupportable. In the case of some, if they loved their neighbors as grudgingly as they love themselves, their gift would be a judgmental curse. But for most of us, can we look at "outsiders" with the same attentiveness with which we face the morning mirror? The same sensitivity to every hint of a lump, every unexplainable pain? But that's what we Christians claim God himself asks of us, and what Jesus manifested in his every word and deed. If that gospel doesn't unnerve you, you've never really heard it.

Genuine love need have nothing to do with feelings or affection or heart palpitations. Love is an act of will, a commitment that takes over when the feelings fail, when the beloved is, at least for now, not even likable. So-called love

songs are not about real love at all, but about being-in-love —
often enamored just of the way the romanticized other makes
me feel. Drained of the misleading stipulations infused into
our understanding of love from the media, the words of Jesus
are no longer as impossible: "I want what's best for you, even
at a cost to myself." That covers not only the intensity of commitment in marriage (which goes a quantum leap beyond the
sexual commitment), but also the easy affection of pals and
friends, sensitivity for acquaintances, and concern even for
the anonymous who are worlds away.

C. S. Lewis knew about love:

> Love anything and your heart will be wrung and pos-
> sibly broken. If you want to make sure of keeping it
> intact you must give it to no one, not even an animal.
> Wrap it carefully round with hobbies and little luxuries;
> avoid all entanglements. Lock it up safe in the casket
> or coffin of your selfishness. But in that casket — safe,
> dark, motionless, airless — it will change. It will not be
> broken; it will become unbreakable, impenetrable, irre-
> deemable. To love is to be vulnerable. The only place
> outside of Heaven where you can be perfectly safe from
> the perturbations of love is Hell. For in hell there is
> no love.

In a talk I once gave to what I believed were almost all
cradle Catholics, I suggested that Jesus didn't allow us the
option of being shy. After all, he told us to climb to the housetops and *shine!* Not much wiggle room there. In the question
period, though, one middle-aged woman argued (somewhat

forcefully) that many Catholics had been trained for a lifetime to be more reserved, and it was unfair for me to ask more. I responded that "reserved" meant something one indeed *had* but held back — out of prudence, reticence, discretion.

*Genuine love need have nothing to do with feelings or affection or heart palpitations. Love is an act of will, a commitment that takes over when the feelings fail, when the beloved is, at least for now, not even likable.*

I said I did honestly resonate with her hesitation, because I myself (who could believe it?) used to be very reticent. But in the toilsome years since, I've become convinced that, despite my manifold shortcomings, God has chosen me, as he did all those stumblers and stammerers in the scripture, like "the stone the builders rejected" (Matt. 21:42), like "the bruised reed he will not break, and a smoldering wick he will not snuff out" (Matt. 12:20). My confidence came not from some conviction of my own native worth but from my conviction of God's confidence in me!

I wasn't claiming everyone should be as incautiously forthright as I am. But I did believe Jesus was asking us to reach beyond what we think is our "limit," that we stand up and be counted at least to the extent our best friends think we are able. I don't believe Jesus asks us to be careless, but he does expect us to *be* fearless — no matter how we *feel*.

There is no room in love for fear. Well-formed love ban-
ishes fear. Since fear is crippling, a fearful life — fear of
death, fear of judgment — is one not yet fully formed in
love. (1 John 4:17)

## The Hardest Love: Forgiveness

In the instances in the four Gospels where Jesus deals one-on-
one with sinners, there is not a single case where he makes the
transgressor crawl, or demands a careful accounting of sins
by species and number, or gives the sinner a compensatory
penance.

In the case of "the woman known as a sinner in the town,"
who wept on his feet and dried them with her hair, she didn't
utter a single syllable, yet Jesus forgave her without hesitation. When his host complained about his lack of discretion,
Jesus said, "I tell you, her many sins have been forgiven —
for she loved much" (Luke 7:47). What a subversion of
values!

When Jesus invited any sinless bystander to be the first to
stone the woman caught in adultery, and they all drifted away
shamefacedly, he said quietly, "Neither do I condemn you. Go
now and leave your life of sin" (John 8:11). The closest he
seems to have come to a penance.

When he asked the many-coupled Samaritan woman at the
well to fetch her husband, and she replied curtly that she had
no husband, Jesus said, "You are right when you say you have
no husband. The fact is, you have had five husbands, and the
man you now have is not your husband. What you have just

said is quite true" (John 4:17–18). Not another word about the casualness of her liaisons, and on he goes to far more important matters, like eternal life: fulfillment, holiness — which apparently were still well within her reach.

Again, in the figure of the father of the prodigal son (Luke 15), Jesus poses what surely is a definitive rejection of any image of God which implies vindictiveness. When the younger son demands "his" half of his father's lifetime work, the father gives it to him, unhesitatingly. When he comes to his senses and trudges home, the father sees him from afar off and runs to the boy — which no Hebrew father would dream of doing. But this father is not hamstrung by customs and traditions. He throws his arms around the boy and kisses him *before* the kid can get out a single word of his carefully memorized confession. He doesn't say, "Before you get back into my house, I want a tally of every specific time and manner you wasted your inheritance!" And instead of a penance, he gives him a party! He even humbles himself to come out to cajole the sullen older son when he's grousing that, like the Pharisees, he'd "played by the rules" without reward. What a lesson in fatherhood, in kindness, in love! What an intimidating model!

At the very end, in Luke's Gospel, when Jesus hung in unspeakable agony after the treatment that so shocked us in *The Passion of the Christ,* the rulers of the people mocked his helplessness, then the soldiers sneered at his kingship, and one of the thieves crucified with him dared him to save himself and them.

> But the other criminal rebuked him. "Don't you fear God," he said, "since you are under the same sentence? We are punished justly, for we are getting what our deeds deserve. But this man has done nothing wrong." Then he said, "Jesus, remember me when you come into your kingdom."                    (Luke 23:40–42)

The man admitted to not a single specific sin, only that he had broken a human law. But despite his own torment, or because of it, he offered his pity for this poor deluded fool. And for that simple kindness, the Son of God sped his entry into paradise.

Finally, it defies our imagination to conceive of Pope John XXIII or Pope John Paul II in blatant apostasy, publicly denying Jesus, bolstered with fierce oaths, and not to an array of inquisitorial torturers but to a couple of *waitresses*! Yet that is precisely what the first pope did do (Matt. 26:69–74). And Jesus still chose him over the wily Judas, the ethereal John, and the worldly wise Matthew. It defies reason.

After the resurrection (John 21), we have no evidence Jesus taxed Peter for his craven denial, not even obliquely, as we just might be tempted to do: "They tell me you were there the night I was being tortured, Pete, ol' buddy!" Instead, in that lovely scene on Lake Tiberias, when Peter spies Jesus waiting on shore with their breakfast, and big-hearted Peter puts clothes *on* to jump into the surf to go to him, Jesus just says, "Come and have breakfast."

Then as they're lounging companionably around the fire, Jesus casually asks, "Simon, son of John, do you truly love me?" Try to imagine the God-sized emptiness in Peter's guts, the pulsing conflict between shame and love, the yearning for the words to compensate. All he can say, helplessly, is, "Lord, you know all things; you know that I love you."

Three times, Jesus asks, and three times Peter answers, the same number of times he had betrayed his friend. And with that trivial recompense — for the sake of Peter's needfulness! — Jesus reinstated him as the first of them. "Feed my lambs. Feed my sheep." Into the hands of this man who had proven himself so imperfect he returned the keys of the Kingdom of God.

After all, Peter had dared to be there that night, when none of the others had. "His sins have been forgiven, for he has loved much." A wrenching reversal of values.

In Luke's Gospel, nearly Jesus' last word in life, just before he forgave the kindly thief and yielded his spirit to his Father, was: "Father, forgive them. They do not know what they're doing!" (Luke 23:34).

Jesus is the model of every confessor, and every Christian. At every Mass the priest quotes Christ: "This is a cup of my blood. . . . It will be shed for you, and for all, so that sins may be forgiven. Do this in memory of me." Not just offer the blood in memory of me, but forgive sins in memory of me. And even more often, each of us has said, "Forgive us our trespasses as we forgive those who trespass against us." It surely does defy reason.

## A Personal Examen

- Has my idea of what being Christian means been warped in any way by the best-intentioned parents and teachers who found the easy-to-hand "Economic Metaphor" the only realistic way to give children even a vague idea of our relationship with God? "Adam and Eve committed a sin so awful that God turned his back on them and refused to love them again till Jesus sneaked down and got himself executed to satisfy God's need for compensation. And of course every time we sin, we incur a debt like that, and it can never be wiped out until we appease God with a studious list of every sin, from the dumbest to the most poisonous." How does that attitude stand up in the face of Jesus' habitual dealings with sinners? The crucifixion? The Last Judgment?

- I find myself in the sandals of the lawyer who challenged Jesus with "And who is my neighbor?" (Luke 10:29) and Peter when he asked if we need to forgive one another seven times (Matt. 18:21). Does Jesus mean to forgive even the callous managers and clients who take me for granted, with not a word of thanks, no matter how hard I work "beyond the call of duty"? The people I've always loved easily — when they get testy, and tiresome, and old? The kids who seem living proof adolescence is incurable?

- On the other hand, doesn't there also come a time for "tough love," when to remain patiently silent is an act of injustice and cowardice? When my friend is mean-spirited in her judgments? When someone at work consistently dodges commitments? When someone is cruelly bullied? When the boss demands something seriously immoral as the cost of my job?

- Perhaps the toughest question: Is it remotely possible that, if I truly loved others in the same way I "love" myself, there would be precious little love of the neighbor in my patch of the woods?

# Chapter Eight

# Perseverance

*Immediately the boy's father exclaimed, "I do believe;*
*help my unbelief!"* —Mark 9:24

I N 1831, a young Illinois man failed in business. The
following year he ran for the state legislature and was
defeated. Another business failed a year later. When he was
twenty-five, he was elected to the legislature, but the next
year his sweetheart died, and he himself suffered a nervous
breakdown in grief. At age twenty-nine, he was defeated for
Speaker of the Legislature and at thirty-four defeated for Congress. At thirty-seven, he was elected to Congress but defeated
two years later. At forty-six, he was defeated for the Senate
and the following year defeated for Vice-President. Defeated
for the Senate again at forty-nine, he was elected President of
the United States two years afterward. The man's name was
Abraham Lincoln.

So it's been through the millennia since Lincoln's namesake,
Abraham of Ur. With only his conviction of God's call to
support him, at age seventy-five, Abram uprooted himself,
his wife, and all his goods, and set off into the unknown.
After over twenty years of more unsubstantiated promises,

the Lord finally graced Abraham with a son, Isaac, only, when the boy was in his teens, to tell the father to sacrifice the son of all those promises! And Abraham was ready to do it. Loyal, persistent, faithful.

*Suffering is a given. Every philosopher from Buddha to Karl Marx began with that primal unfairness. All the world's creation myths struggled with the enigma of a wise and benevolent Creator but a life any fool could have designed more leniently.*

Rather than the wrathful image of Yahweh so persistent in our imaginations (more from biblical movies than from the scriptures), the more common sense of religion (our connection to God) in the Old Testament is the metaphor of the marriage covenant, forged at the birth of the Hebrew nation on Mount Sinai. The analogy is most apt, because a marriage — or any relationship, even with God — is not a single act of faith. Rather, it is a process. Those vowed to one another after thirty years are a lot more married than on their wedding day. The same is true of the history of Yahweh with the inconstant Israel, from the Garden of Eden to the desert where the Baptist awaited his time. Yahweh is consistently the bridegroom, helplessly ardent as in the mostly hushed-up "Song of Songs," the longsuffering spouse in Hosea who waits outside his beloved's bordello for her to come to her senses and return to him.

Homilists are fond of asking us to appreciate how truly persevering God has been with us, remaining faithful even after we've gone awhoring after the Baals, time and time again. But I risk the Inquisition here to ask the obverse question, rarely broached: How long are we expected to persist with a God who ambushes us with tragedy, often just as we've achieved some equanimity after the last unwelcome surprise? How do we capture a God who invented not only breathtaking sunsets but emphysema? The April showers that bring May flowers but also tsunamis? The innocent gurgle of infants and the fanatic screams of suicide bombers?

As Robert Frost said so laconically: "Forgive, O Lord, my little jokes on Thee, and I'll forgive Thy Great Big Joke on me."

## Suffering

In the broadest sense of the word, "suffering" means giving up something we love or care for or even are just comfortable with. In that sense, getting out of bed is suffering, leaving behind the warm cocoon of the covers and the unbothered serenity of sleep to face the burdens and mishaps and irritating expectations of the day. The point of most stories and biographies in our libraries is that suffering is the only path of growth as a human being, that there is a purpose to human suffering *if* we rise to the challenge.

Suffering is a given. Every philosopher from Buddha to Karl Marx began with that primal unfairness. All the world's creation myths struggled with the enigma of a wise and benevolent Creator but a life any fool could have designed more leniently. To understand, for instance, the inequity of sexuality, which expects one half of the race to suffer menstruation, pregnancy, labor, nursing, and menopause, while the other half gets off scot free, some myths imagine the Creator's intention was that all humans be born hermaphrodites and bear the sexual burden equally (as in Ursula LeGuin's *The Left Hand of Darkness*). But some rebels escaped the original environment too early; thus the imbalance — not the flawless Creator's fault but the insubordination of his creatures. In our Judeo-Christian story, the unfairness is rooted in the suspicion that the female fell first. Once her mate joined her in her rebellion, we have an explanation for our idyllic dreams (the fodder of travel agents) of paradisal islands where the food drops off the trees and no one has to work or be watchful. However, *The Lord of the Flies* embodies the lie at the core of those hopes: Once you put humans anywhere, they will screw up.

## Legitimate and Unmerited Suffering

We can sort out suffering in several different ways. One way isolates what some term "legitimate suffering" from "unmerited suffering." Once one grants a purposeful Creator, whose basic purpose for humans is to train their souls — to invite free evolution beyond basic animal nature by surmounting predictable obstacles — then each natural crisis in physical growth is an invitation to a broader and deeper participation in being human, preparing oneself to be capable of the autonomy of life without parents and then for the joys of heaven. Those trials are what Hamlet called "the thousand natural shocks that flesh is heir to." Seen in that perspective, such trials as adolescence are certainly unpleasant but "legitimate," more readily understandable.

*Who can satisfactorily justify a God who can allow cancer to cut down a saint? Or allow his only Son to be insulted, scourged, and executed?*

Unmerited suffering is discomfort for which no individual was responsible for causing: My parents broke up, my doctor says I have cancer, a fire destroyed my whole neighborhood, my best friend betrayed my confidence, someone of another race beat me out for "my" scholarship, my mother's an alcoholic. None of them my fault, but I have to live with them or go mad trying to make the truth be not-true.

### Physical and Moral Suffering

Another way to study our common burden subdivides unmerited suffering. *Physical* suffering (or physical "evil") — hurricanes, cancer, death itself — are the conditions involved in living in this world rather than another. No human is responsible for them, only Whoever set up this environment with these pitfalls. The alternate type of innocent suffering is *moral* evil: "Man's inhumanity to man" — war, murder, rape, robbery. These are a direct result of human will and perversity, freely degrading oneself or others to the level of animals or vegetables or stepping stones. Although this places the rebel human will as the *immediate* cause of such suffering, it doesn't let the kindly Creator off the hook. If such a Person is, indeed, the *Ultimate* Cause, He/She/It made the decision to give wits and freedom to an inadequately evolved tribe of apes. Some thoughtful people find that so contradictory they deny such a Cause can exist.

Each of us, by the mere fact of being born (for which none of us was responsible), is condemned to death. Samuel Beckett's *Waiting for Godot* makes that absurdity curtly clear: "Astride of a grave and a difficult birth. Down in the hole, lingeringly, the grave-digger puts on the forceps." And the existentialist novelist Albert Camus tells us that in a godless universe, the two greatest curses are intelligence and hope: hungers we endure, by our very human nature, for answers and survival, in a world where neither exists. Better to be a pig that never asks why or yearns to outwit death. It's a bravely honest stance, but deadly cold.

Blackouts and DTs for someone who abuses alcohol and the human liver have a clear cause-effect relationship. Choose the one, you reflexively "choose" the other. What is far more difficult to comprehend is suffering for which one is in no way culpable and which seems to have no evident redemptive purpose. Who can satisfactorily justify a God who can allow cancer to cut down a saint? Or allow his only Son to be insulted, scourged, and executed?

The whole question that underlies the book of Job is the mystery of suffering for which the victim is in no way responsible. According to the book's premise, God allows the subjection of Job, "the perfect and upright man," to one physical and moral evil after another. Natural disasters and evil marauders destroy his children, his animals, his crops. His skin is caked with boils, and even his wife deserts him. Yet despite his friends' orthodox insistence that God makes only the guilty suffer, Job knows unarguably he has never done anything nearly wicked enough to justify suffering such as his.

Dostoevsky's Ivan Karamazov was tormented by the same blatant inequity:

> Tell me yourself, I challenge your answer. Imagine that you are creating a fabric of human destiny with the object of making men happy in the end, giving them peace and rest at last, but that it was essential and inevitable to torture to death only one tiny creature — that baby beating its breast with its fist, for instance — and to found that edifice on its unavenged tears, would you consent to be the architect on those conditions? Tell me, and tell the truth.

### Legitimate Suffering

Legitimate suffering, as its designation suggests, is the easiest to accept, even though it is painful. In that broad sense of "suffering" (a loss in the hope of better) any work is suffering, a forfeiture of freedom for a felt purpose: a paycheck, the well-being of one's family, a sense of being useful. Living together — from a married couple to a family to a community — is suffering: forswearing independence, curbing resentments, compromising, because we can accomplish more together than alone. Wind sprints and weightlifting are painful, but suffered for a purpose, athletic or cosmetic. Learning is suffering, disciplining oneself to persevere with few immediate rewards, which is why so little of it occurs, since those on whom it is inflicted find no felt purpose in enduring it. Seeing a purpose counteracts the suffering, gives it meaning.

Any significant change in one's life is, in its broadest sense, suffering: a loss. Growth itself is suffering, since we have to give up a self we were comfortable with in order to evolve a better self. Such losses-that-invite-growth consistently intrude on human life, what Erik Erikson called "natural disequilibriums."

Birth itself is the first. For nine months in the womb we were in paradise: warm, fed, floating, free of all care because we couldn't think. Then through no fault of our own, we were ejected, and our first birthday present was a slap on the butt. But without it, we'd die.

Then, just as we got things comfy again, parents started intruding with weaning and potty training, which were unnerving. But without them we'd never achieve physical independence — which was worth the loss. Then Mommy shoved us out to play with the other snotty kids, even in the cold! But without it, we'd never have learned how to settle disputes without an adult arbitrator — worth the loss. Then the terrible betrayal at the kindergarten doorway! Stranding us with all those strangers! But without it, we'd lack skills to survive in the world on our own — worth the loss. Then adolescence, when bodies we'd taken for granted for so long began to betray us. But without it, we could never achieve personal identity — worth the loss.

Marriage is "suffering," giving up the swinging bachelor life to promise responsibility for another person. But without it you face all challenges alone — worth the loss. Having children surrenders the hard-won intimacy and partnership of marriage to allow in an intruder, to whom you commit yourself to raise a quarter million dollars, sight unseen! But without it, the two of you have nothing but yourselves to spark excitement in your life, without the uninvited challenges that keep us growing — which is what our humanity invites.

But since we live in an ethos that recoils even from inconvenience, much less the troublesome effort to change one's stultifying habits, it's not surprising we live in a society composed in great part of terminal adolescents. One can pretend to "solve" the question of legitimate suffering — loss inflicted on everyone since the Cro-Magnons — either by evading it or by suppressing knowledge of it.

Psychiatrist Carl Jung insists that evading legitimate suffering, arising simply from dealing with the world we were dealt, always ends in neurosis: anxiety, obsessions, narcissism, blaming our faults on our personalities rather than blaming our personalities on our faults. "I'm lazy" seems self-justifying, as if it were an incurable disease of which I am a victim. But living an illusion, lying to oneself and believing the lies, is very hard work. Thus, what we accept as a substitute for the truth becomes more painful than accepting the truth. What's more, denying the suffering that comes from facing life as it is, flat on, avoids growth as a human being, since growth is by definition leaving the security of the cocoon in order to fly. And when we avoid deeper humanity, we avoid holiness, the will of God for us.

Suppressing suffering involved in facing the truth — drowning it in booze or drugs or witless busyness, "enduring" what is objectively changeable — is equally self-destructive. Perhaps the most widespread neurosis is minding one's own business, sticking the thumb in the mouth and letting the rest of the world go by, grudging with one's attention, affection, time, and money. As Burger, the psychiatrist in *Ordinary People*, said, "If you can't feel pain, you're not going to feel anything else, either."

## Moral Evil

The result of what even unbelievers designate "original sin," that is, the human penchant for inflicting suffering, even on oneself, is called *moral* evil. We are the only species tempted, or even able, to act in contradiction to its own God-given nature. Whatever its historical causes, the result is incontrovertible, the only doctrine immediately evident from the morning papers. If God chose to give freedom to a tribe of apes, moral (human) evil was a foregone conclusion.

Clearly, if all that exists takes its existence from a benevolent God, and if we accept that, when "God saw all that he had made, and it was very good" (Gen. 1:31), then the brains he gifted us with are meant to discern, insofar as we're able, what that purpose is.

As we saw, what differentiates us from other animals seems to be our capacity to keep deepening our abilities to learn and love. Yet both of those are merely potential. The Creator freely invented a species that can frustrate his plans! There is a very important clue to his personality: He finally got to creating a creature who is free, which is alarmingly generous. Unlike ourselves, who find it so difficult to avoid jealousy when those we love also love others, even more than they love us, this God was willing to take that risk.

*God finds no objection to our railing at him, even wrestling with him as Jacob did, even bawling him out for a fare-thee-well, using every curse word in our arsenal as we would with any other lifelong friend — as long as, when we've calmed down, we forgive God because of all the good times. For truly the good times have far outnumbered and outweighed the bad times.*

Tristan and Iseult were rapturously in love with one another only because they'd ingested a love potion. No matter how tragic their agonies, it was ersatz love from the start, not the real thing. Genuine love is meaningless without freedom, when the other is helpless *not* to love me. In that way, we can romanticize, as even the Bible writers do, that mountains and trees and beasts offer love and praise and obedience to their Maker. But in reality, they have no choice. Only we do.

Then we must have a true option to choose wrongly. We also must be able to choose less well. In order for heroism to have any meaning whatever, cowardice must be a realistic alternative. If celibacy is to be a genuine gift to God, sexual fulfillment must be an honestly compelling option, not a flight from commitment or a disgust with our incarnation.

With that understanding, experience of suffering — across the spectrum of its meanings — is *essential!* Who could value the dawn without fear of the dark? Who would exult in good health if we had never been sick? Moreover, who would feel *grateful* unless all happiness were precarious? "Shall we take good from God and not trouble?" (Job 2:10).

## Unmerited Suffering

Whether one suffers from the vagaries of the environment (physical evil) or from the others' callous use of their freedom (moral evil), the "answer" is the same. It comes at the end of the book of Job, but it is not "fair" or "just." Nor is it, in any strict sense, an answer. In the first place, when God finally arrives to respond to Job's accusations of mistreatment, God turns up in a whirlwind, which is not exactly even-handed. But that is God's whole point. Job's situation is not a question of justice but a matter of trust. In the second place, the "answer" is not rational at all, but rather a person-to-Person experiential encounter between a Creator and his creature.

"Brace yourself like a man," says the imperious voice from the windstorm. "I will question you, and you shall answer me. Where were you when I laid the earth's foundation? Tell me, if you understand" (Job 38:3–4).

In effect, God is saying, "Have you forgotten who I AM and who you are? Is there some ground on which you presume I should check my plans with you first? Is it just possible I could have reasons your space-time mind is incapable of fathoming?"

The "patience of Job" is a cliché. If it means fidelity despite boundless doubt, then Job, like Abraham, was a patient, trusting man. But if "patience" means unquestioning silent acquiescence, he was not at all patient. For thirty-seven chapters he relentlessly challenges the unthinking orthodoxy of his four friends who insist he must be guilty. Therefore, since scripture is the word of God, and Job is rewarded in the end for his perseverance, God himself seems to have no problem with our using the wits he gave us even to challenge him. (There is a wonderful Jewish suggestion that, when we do use our God-given wits to dispute with him, God dances for joy!)

God finds no objection to our railing at him, even wrestling with him as Jacob did, even bawling him out for a fare-thee-well, using every curse word in our arsenal as we would with any other lifelong friend — as long as, when we've calmed down, we forgive God because of all the good times. For truly the good times have far outnumbered and outweighed the bad times.

Very often in classes, especially with all boys, I find fierce resistance. If you argue the patent differences between human sex and animal sex, you can tell instantly who the sexually active students are, because they defend a vested interest with no pretense at a fair interchange. At those times, I say, "Look, don't be mad at me because I know more than you do, because I've read more than you have, because I've given these questions more thought than you."

That's at least remotely like our crying, "Unfair!" to the very Person who gave us the means to see inequity and the skills to voice our objections. Therefore, if forgiveness is the hardest loving, perhaps the way in which we love God most profoundly is forgiving God for *being* God, for having reasons and a perspective we are simply, humblingly unable to grasp.

## Attitude

Wisdom is making peace with the unchangeable. We have the freedom to face the unavoidable with dignity, to understand the transformational value that *attitude* works on suffering. Are we responsible for our unmerited sufferings? The answer is no. And yes. We are not responsible for our predicament as its cause — whether it be cancer or job loss or the death of a child or spouse. But we are responsible for what we *do* with the effects, with what we build from the rubble Fate has made of our lives.

Psychiatrist Viktor Frankl, who survived the Nazi camps, in his book *Man's Search for Meaning*, echoes Nietzsche: "Whoever has a *why* to live for can bear with almost any *how.*" Anyone who could cling to his or her own inalienable soul — by clinging to even the memory of a loved one, a life-goal, a belief in any understanding of a purposive God — could survive.

> Is [the prisoner] still spiritually responsible for what is happening to him psychically, for what the concentration camp has "made" of him? Our answer is: he is. For even in this socially limited environment, in spite of this societal restriction upon his personal freedom, the ultimate freedom remains his: the freedom even in the camp to give some shape to his existence.

The ultimate freedom is the *attitude* with which we face unpleasant challenges. But it is a freedom. We can settle for mere survival.

The only hand we have to play is the hand Fate deals us. We need not be victims of our *biological* fate. Stephen Hawking is a good example of a Phoenix risen from ashes. One night the evening news reported a young man receiving his Eagle Scout award. Nothing newsworthy in that, except he was twenty-two and couldn't give an acceptance speech. Instead, his father spoke it as his son pointed to letters on a board atop his wheelchair. He had cerebral palsy. For his merit badge in hiking, he had pushed his chair nine miles, then crawled the rest of the way.

We need not be victims of our *psychological* fate. We are, surely, driven by the winds, but a skillful sailor can use the wind, whereas "I'm doomed" or "I'm nobody" become self-fulfilling prophecies. As Frankl starkly and firmly asserts: "A faulty upbringing exonerates nobody." Those with callous fostering in shoddy circumstances are in truth victims of others' mistakes, but it is the inescapable burden they were delivered, and they are no more hamstrung by it than the boy with cerebral palsy. Each of our stories is unique, with its own demons and dragons. Accept that and get on with what you have left: you.

We need not be victims of our *situational* fate, immured in its "laws," living a makeshift existence, settling for mere "survival." People who went down on the *Titanic* went down singing. People have gotten off third-generation welfare. Women and men survived Dachau, Auschwitz, the Gulag, Teheran, Bosnia, Darfur. And they came through battered but unbowed, with their own souls clasped firmly in their own hands. If such heroism is possible for so many ordinary people, surely it is possible to say no to soulless societies and soulless selves, to the nay-sayers and nobodies we're surrounded by. Surely it is possible to say no to the values purveyed incessantly by the media.

Here is a meaning to "value" totally unfamiliar in a utilitarian society where "dignity, integrity, altruism" simply don't compute. How much do they pay? But in a lifeview where one's character is more indicative of worth than one's bank balance, the fighting alone counts. There is no lost cause if the cause is just. In the going, I'm already there.

Dr. Martin Luther King Jr. wrote: "The value of unmerited suffering [calls us] either to react with bitterness or seek to transform the suffering into a creative force. If only to save myself from bitterness, I have attempted to see my personal ordeals as an opportunity to transfigure myself and heal the people involved in the tragic situation which now obtains. I have lived these last few years with the conviction that unearned suffering is redemptive."

What suffering — accepted with an attitude of challenge — redeems us from is our misplaced feeling of uselessness, of meaninglessness, of being dismissible as human beings.

Only two alternatives: rise to the challenge or drown in self-pity.

Aesop's fable about the turtle and the hare remains true: "Slow and steady wins the race." As Aristotle wrote, as with any other virtue, one learns perseverance by persevering.

## Jesus' Passion

Personally, I find iron obstacles between the Father revealed by Jesus in the parable of the prodigal son and the image of God propounded for centuries by theologians who required Jesus' sufferings as an "atonement" for sins. I have contrarious difficulties with Jesus as a "ransom" for us to an offended and unbending God.

The God revealed in Jesus' unvarying treatment of sinners — the woman who wept on his feet, the adulterous woman, the Samaritan woman at the well, the cowardly Peter, the kindly thief crucified with him — gives uncritical *acceptance*. Never a need to crawl, to list every sin by species and number, to fulfill a compensatory penance. How do I square that kindly Father with a vindictive God who demands blood-money in recompense for two simpletons (whom he himself gave the freedom to rebel) eating a fictional piece of fruit? How could the God who asks us to forgive seventy times seven times hold a grudge so long?

Note well: I do not deny that centuries-old teaching. I merely state my quite fallible reluctance to accept it readily. Not even a fool could deny the effects of "original sin." But I do balk at using the Economic Metaphor, the almost irreparable stain of indebtedness, to explain human inconstancy. Isn't ransom paid only to a *hostile* power?

I have enormous difficulty harmonizing the God embodied in Jesus and the fault-finding God I learned of in my childhood, youth, and young manhood. I accept that those two seemingly incompatible views must have a way of co-existing, but I have yet to discover it.

However, among those for whom the enormous degradation the Son of God endured for us has not been deadened by repetition, I wonder if we can find a depth in it beyond atonement. In his forthright confrontation with evil and suffering, Christ did indeed free us — from *fear:* fear that our sins might be beyond forgiveness, fear that without resurrection from death our lives have no meaning or purpose, fear that no one except a few loved ones truly cares. To my mind, that liberation comes not from God's acceptance of an infinite propitiation but in the very nature of a God who *is* Love, who dotes on us not despite our faults or because of our good deeds but because we are his. Such love is beyond any science, even theology.

The baffling anomaly of an omnipotent God, by nature inaccessible to anything even negative, much less helpless agony — *the God of Job!* — willingly yielding to degradation defies rational explanation! To those not dulled to it by repetition, the cross staggers the mind. What could motivate such abasement? The only answer is no rational answer: love, freely given, prompted by nothing more than a Father's deathless infatuation.

The Passion declares: "Here! Look! Is this enough to prove how important you are to me? If wonderment at the carousal of the universe doesn't prove it, if the thousands of years of my faithful waiting outside your bordello doors for you isn't enough, is *this* enough? Does this demonstrate to you that you are too precious to degrade yourselves with the Baals, the momentary bread-and-circuses, the ersatz pleasures that tempt you so easily?"

Bewildering as that love is, it is more comprehensible, and more congruous with the God embodied in the words and actions of Jesus, than the God placated by blood sacrifice, as was most understandable and accepted in a barbarian world. What's more, it checkmates the two basest motives for moral behavior: fear and hope of reward, what Lawrence Kohlberg called "preconventional morality," tooth and fang, survival of the fittest. It also "allows" of a God who goes beyond even "conventional morality," group loyalty and law and order, quid pro quo, the just balance. It provides a model of "post-conventional" motivation: altruism that is not rational but beyond rational. Difficult as it might be for those whose scope is at those lower levels, this is the God "in whose image" we are fashioned, invited beyond the self-centered animal, invited even beyond the self-governed human, invited into the Trinity Family. Into holiness.

## A Personal Examen

- How much of my understanding of God and my relationship to God (my religion) is still rooted in and limited by the explanations and understandings accessible to a child or teenager, stages when I left behind any formal religious exploration? Am I really *more* Christian than I was then? How much is curbed by the level at which most homilists feel constrained to preach? If the evolution of my soul has been circumscribed by years of involvement in real and more urgently pressing issues, what ought I to do about that, concretely, specifically?

- Look at a crucifix. Reflect on whom that corpse embodied. The Architect of the Universe, compacted into that bleeding mass. Can I honestly say, and accept in the depths of myself: "Yes, it's inescapable. I am worth that."

*"Truly a spirituality for the 21st century!"*
— *Dolores Leckey*

# Catholic Spirituality for Adults

### General Editor
### Michael Leach

Forthcoming volumes include:

- *Charity* by Virgil Elizondo
- *Listening to God's Word* by Alice Camille
- *Community* by Adela Gonzalez
- *Incarnation* by John Shea
- And many others.

To learn more about forthcoming titles in the series, go to *orbisbooks.com*.

For free study guides and discussion ideas on this book, go to
*http://www.rclbenziger.com.*

Please support your local bookstore.

Thank you for reading *Holiness* by William J. O'Malley. We hope you found it beneficial.